The Flute, How It Works

The Flute, How It Works

A Practical Guide to Flute Ownership

Michael J. Pagliaro

Co-Published in Partnership with the
National Association for Music Education

ROWMAN & LITTLEFIELD
Lanham • Boulder • New York • London

Published by Rowman & Littlefield
An imprint of The Rowman & Littlefield Publishing Group, Inc.
4501 Forbes Boulevard, Suite 200, Lanham, Maryland 20706
www.rowman.com

86-90 Paul Street, London EC2A 4NE

Copyright © 2024 by The Rowman & Littlefield Publishing Group, Inc.

All rights reserved. No part of this book may be reproduced in any form or by any electronic or mechanical means, including information storage and retrieval systems, without written permission from the publisher, except by a reviewer who may quote passages in a review.

British Library Cataloguing in Publication Information Available

Library of Congress Cataloging-in-Publication Data

ISBN: 978-1-5381-9076-0 (pbk.)
ISBN: 978-1-5381-9077-7 (ebook)

Table of Contents

Acknowledgments iv

Introduction v

1. What Are the Parts of My Flute? 1

2. How Does My Flute Work? 5

3. What Are the Different Kinds of Flutes? 11

4. How Are Flutes Made? 17

5. How Do I Take Care of My Flute? 25

6. How Should I Plan My Practice Sessions? 35

7. A Survey of the History of Woodwind Instruments 39

8. What Items (Accessories) Will I Need to Help Me Play My Flute? 61

Appendix 69

The Science of Sound 69
Glossary of Woodwind Instrument Terms 75
Dictionary of Flute Terms 81
Index of Flute Parts 83
Instrument Ownership Record 85

Index 91

Acknowledgments

The following extraordinarily gifted musical instrument fabrication and distribution professionals have generously granted permission to use information and artwork from their websites. Listed in alphabetical order, they are:

Burkart Flutes and Piccolos, www.burkhart.com

Donna Altieri Bags, info@altieribags.com

Erick D. Brand, for permission to show the clarinet key system diagram from the Erick D. Brand Band Instrument Repair Manual

The Gemeinhardt Company, the world's largest maker of flutes

How It's Made, https://www.sciencechannel.com/show/how-its-made-flute

Lars Kirmser, publisher and musical instrument specialist at http://www.musictrader.com

Rick Wilson, for permission to use his Historical Flute Page at http://www.oldflutes.com/boehm.htm

Introduction

The method book you are now using was written to help you learn how to play the flute. That book contains information on holding your flute, making a sound, reading music, playing different notes, and much more.

This book will teach you additional information about your instrument to help you better understand how it works, how to work it, care for it, and how to be a more knowledgeable flutist.

The first section of this book reviews information that might be on the first few pages of your method book. Even if you know that information, spend a few moments reading this section to see if you can find something you have not yet learned. You will be learning information about the flute that not many students will ever know.

You do not have to read this book in the order in which the chapters appear. Start at any chapter that interests you, and then, as you progress, move to the chapters related to your flute studies. Because you can read any chapter, some needed information is repeated to cover the issue under study.

NOTE: In music, the term head joint can also be written as one word. You might see it as headjoint.

Chapter 1

What Are the Parts of My Flute?

Keep your flute with you when reading this chapter, and follow the descriptions. A flute has three main parts. Pictured below, from left to right, are the foot joint, body, and head joint.

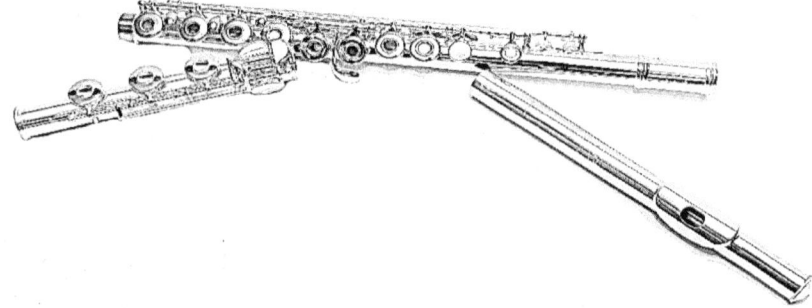

A flute is about 26 ½ inches long and looks like this when put together.

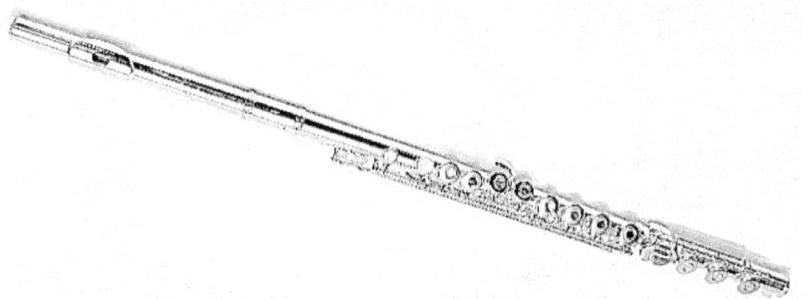

Added to those three main parts are the keys you can see on the flute's body and several other parts you cannot see. These parts are in the head joint.

Flute Head Joint— Your flute head joint is a tube with a lip plate (A) and an embouchure hole (B). The lip plate also called the embouchure plate, is designed to support your lower lip when in a playing position. The embouchure hole is the place where you produce the sound. (More on this in chapter 2.)

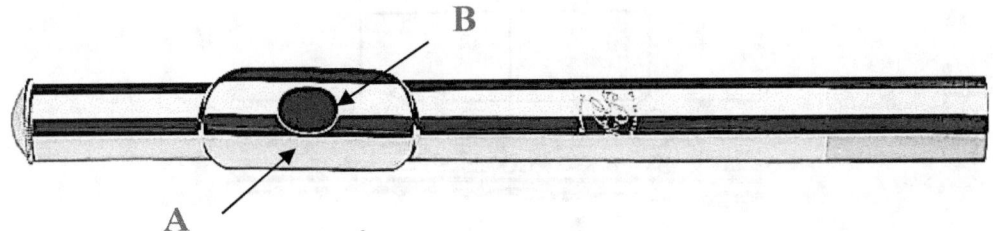

Flute Head Joint

1

Pictured below are the parts that are inside the head joint. Beginning from the left side, there is a crown (A), screw (B), first metal plate (C), cork (D), and second metal plate (E). Combined, they are called the crown assembly. The crown assembly can be moved in and out of the head joint and is used to tune your flute. You will read more about tuning in chapter 2.

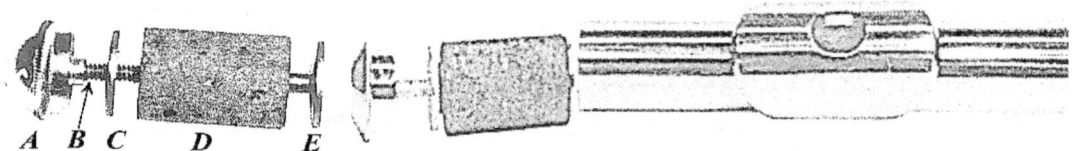

Crown Assembly

Tone Holes—The body and foot joint of the flute form a tube with a number of holes called tone holes. Look under the keys of your flute to see the tone holes.

Below is a picture of a flute body without keys so you can see the tone holes clearly. Here, you can see the posts sticking up from the body and wire springs attached to those posts. The posts hold the keys in place, and the wire springs make the keys return to position after you press and release them.

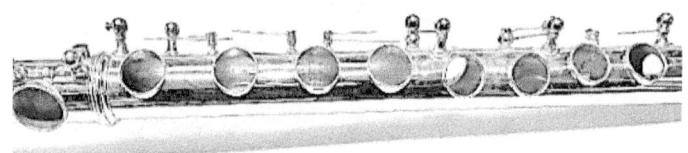

Flute Body Without Keys

The Key System—The three parts of a flute key are the spatula (A), which is the part in contact with your finger. The pad cup (B) has a pad to cover the tone hole, and the arm (C) connects the spatula and pad cup.

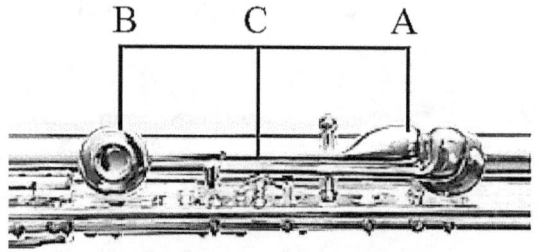

Parts of a Flute Key

2

Key Springs—Each key is connected to a spring, which returns the key to its original position after you press and release it. Two types of springs are wire and flat springs, both pictured below. Look under the keys on your flute to see the springs.

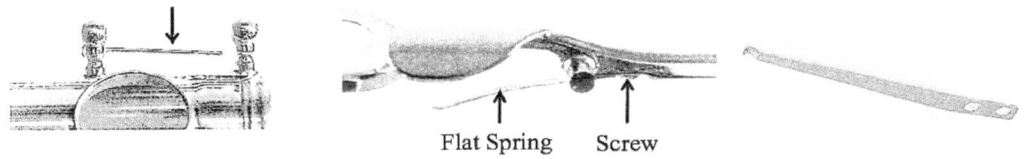

Wire and Flat Key Springs

Plateau or Closed Hole Keys—Flutes can have two different types of keys. If you are a young player, your flute probably has keys that fully cover the tone holes. These are called plateau keys or closed-hole keys. The picture below on the left shows plateau keys.

Open Hole Keys—The picture on the right shows keys with a hole in their center. These are called open-hole keys and are usually found on more expensive flutes. When you play an open-hole flute, you must be sure that your finger pad covers the open hole completely. Some players believe an open-hole flute will produce a richer sound than a closed-hole flute. Not everyone agrees with that idea.

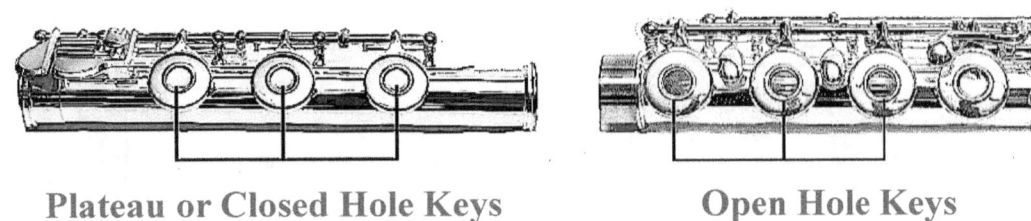

Plateau or Closed Hole Keys   **Open Hole Keys**

Different Flute Key Systems—Some flutes have slightly different key systems. Look at your flute's G key. This key can be in line with the other keys, or it can be slightly offset. In the picture below, notice how the G key is in line with the other keys in the first picture and offset in the second picture.

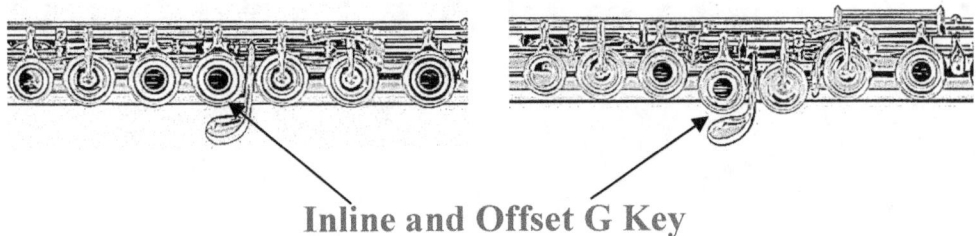

Inline and Offset G Key

A flute with an offset key has a shorter distance to reach and is used on some student flutes. The inline G key is a bit longer to reach and would be easier for a player with longer fingers. Some feel that the offset G key is a better choice for players who perform for long periods since there is less stress on the shorter reach.

Low B Key—Student-level flutes are most commonly built with C4 (1 line below the treble clef staff) as their lowest note. Some flutes extend that lowest note, even one note lower, too low Bb3. (See Scientific Pitch Notation on page 69.)

Advanced flutists should have a low Bb key, which is not usually needed for a beginner. Professional model flutes can have a range as low as A3 (two lines below the treble clef staff). Below are pictures of a flute foot joint with the low C and B keys.

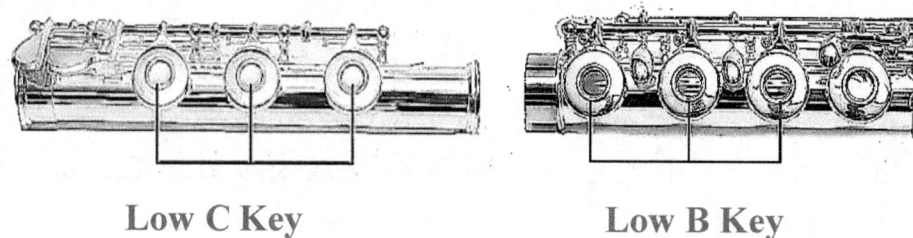

Low C Key   **Low B Key**

Chapter 2

How Does My Flute Work?

Sound Production—In your first lesson, you learned to produce a sound on your flute by placing the lip plate against your chin just below your lower lip and directing a stream of air across the embouchure hole, as pictured below.

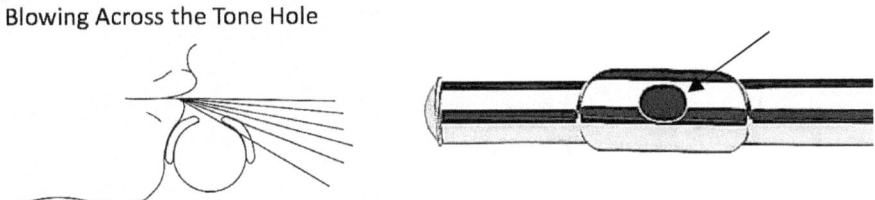

Producing a Sound

As the air stream strikes the edge of the embouchure hole opposite your lips, the air stream waves above and below that edge. This motion causes the air inside your flute to vibrate and make a sound.

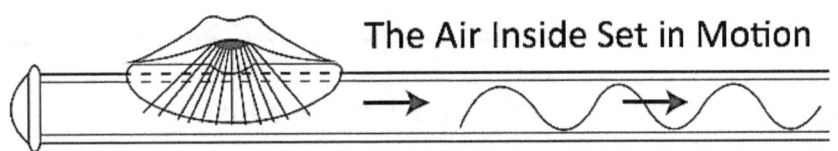

When you close or open the tone holes, by pressing or releasing the keys, you shorten or lengthen the vibrating column of air in the body of your flute. The length of that vibrating column produces the note you are playing. That vibrating column of air will reach the first open tone hole on your flute's body. There, the vibration stops.

The arrow in the picture of the flute below shows the distance from the embouchure hole to the first open tone hole on the flute's body. As you close the holes, that distance increases, lowering the notes. A shorter vibrating air column produces a high pitch. A longer vibrating air column will produce a lower pitch.

First Open Tone Hole

Flute Head Joint— Pictured below is the crown assembly described in chapter 1. To Review, beginning from the left side, there is a crown (A), screw (B), first metal plate (C), cork (D), and second metal plate (E). Combined, they are called the crown assembly.

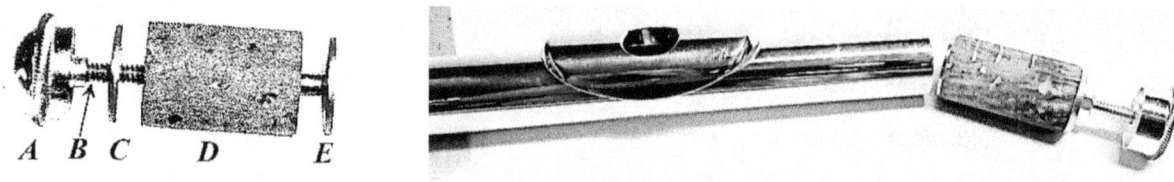

Crown Assembly

The crown assembly can be moved in or out and is used to tune your flute. Look carefully at the non-slotted end of your cleaning rod, and you will see a mark near the end of the rod.

Cleaning Rod Tuning Slot

This mark is a guide to help you tune your flute. Place the tuning rod in the head joint so the mark on the tuning rod is visible through the embouchure hole. Your flute should be in tune when that mark is in the center of the embouchure hole.

If the mark is not in the center of the embouchure hole, adjust the crown assembly in to raise the pitch or out to lower the pitch. To do so, loosen the crown screw and move it in or out, so the cleaning rod mark is on center. This adjustment is for general tuning. Ask your teacher to help with this the first time you do it.

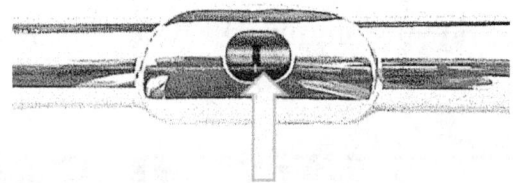

Tuning Rod in Embouchure Hole

Fingering—On an open hole flute, the six tone holes are covered by each hand's index, middle, and third fingers. On a closed hole flute, those same keys are covered by padded keys, which you press with the same fingering pattern. All other tone holes are covered by keys, which you operate with your thumb and pinky finger of each hand. Put the correct fingers in the correct place at the correct time, and you make music.

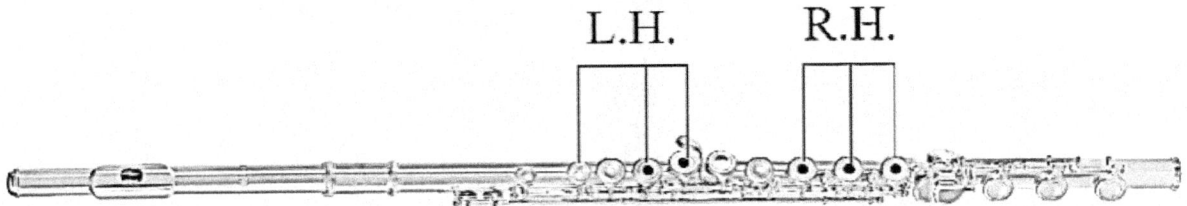

Review—Sound is produced on your flute when you blow a stream of air across the embouchure hole in the head joint. That air stream sets the air in the flute's body into motion, producing a sound. You can change that sound by pressing and releasing the keys on the flute's body.

The following pages have diagrams showing the flute key system, where your fingers are placed on a flute, and a basic fingering chart for the C flute.

Concert Flute in C Key System

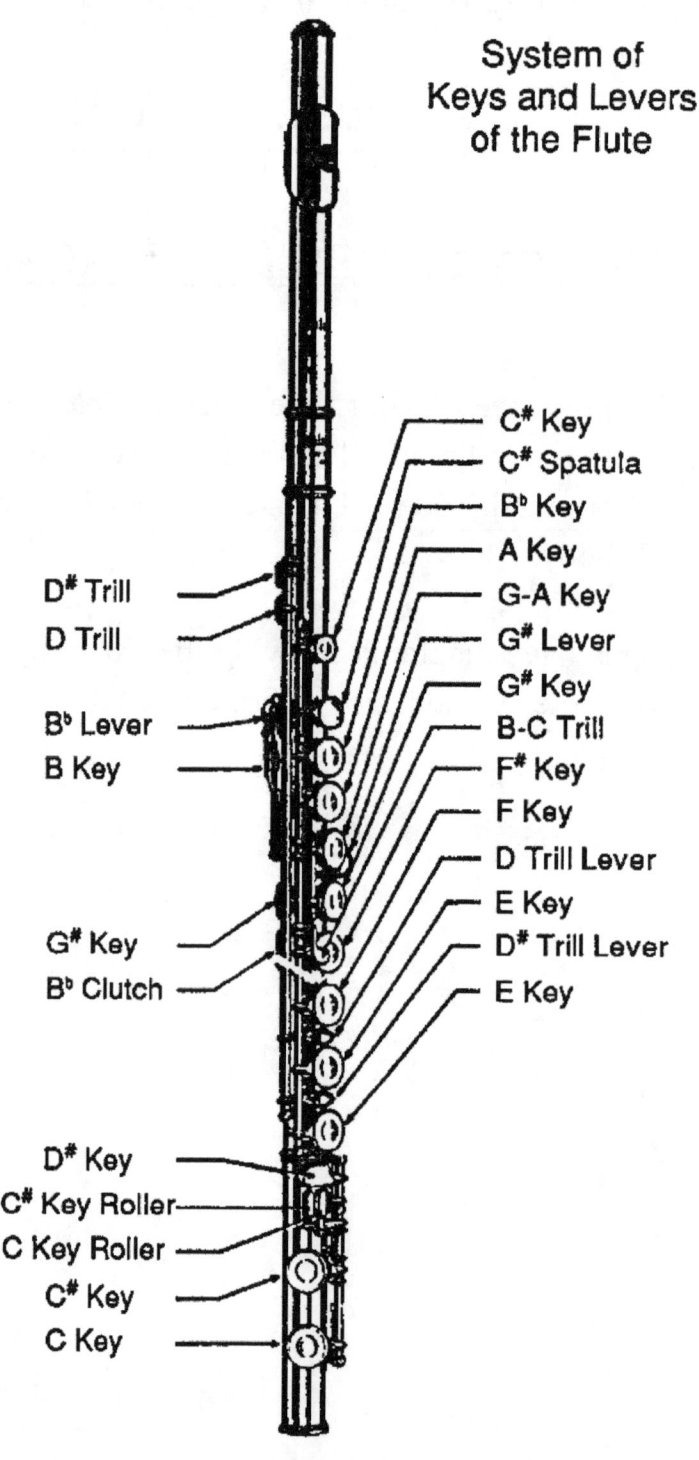

The diagram below shows the keys of a flute and how they can be represented on a flute fingering chart.

Finger Placement of Flute Keys

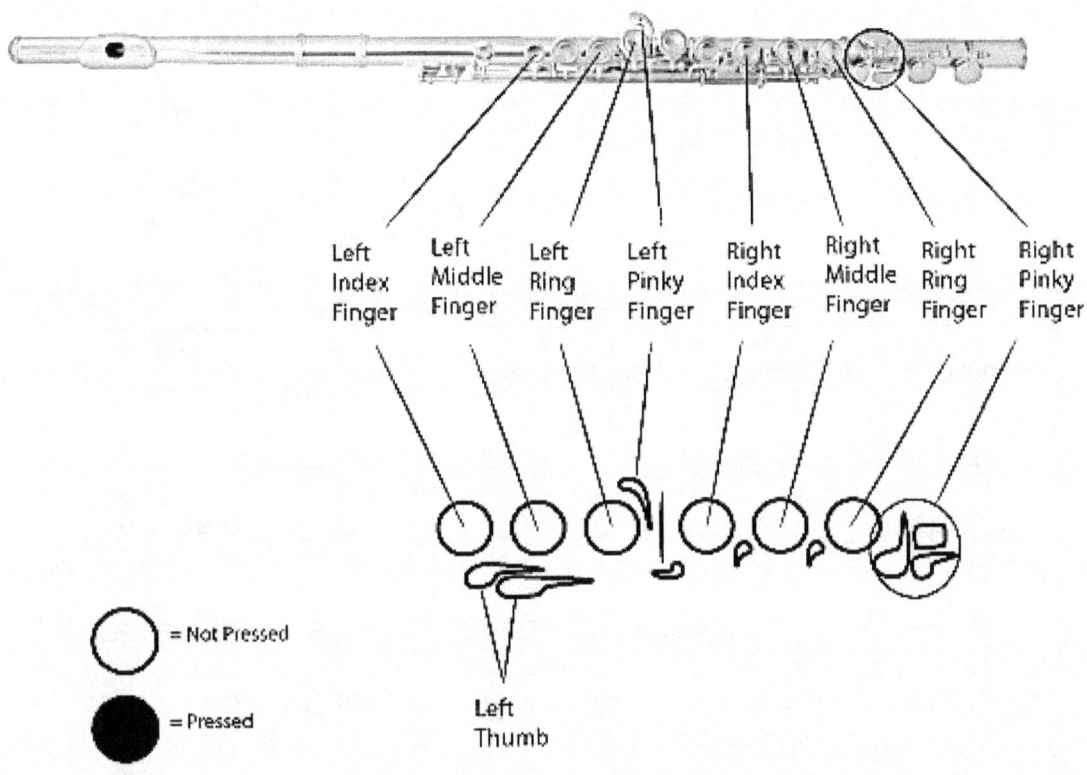

Basic Flute Fingering Chart

To finger a note, press the filled-in keys or levers indicated in the diagram below the note.

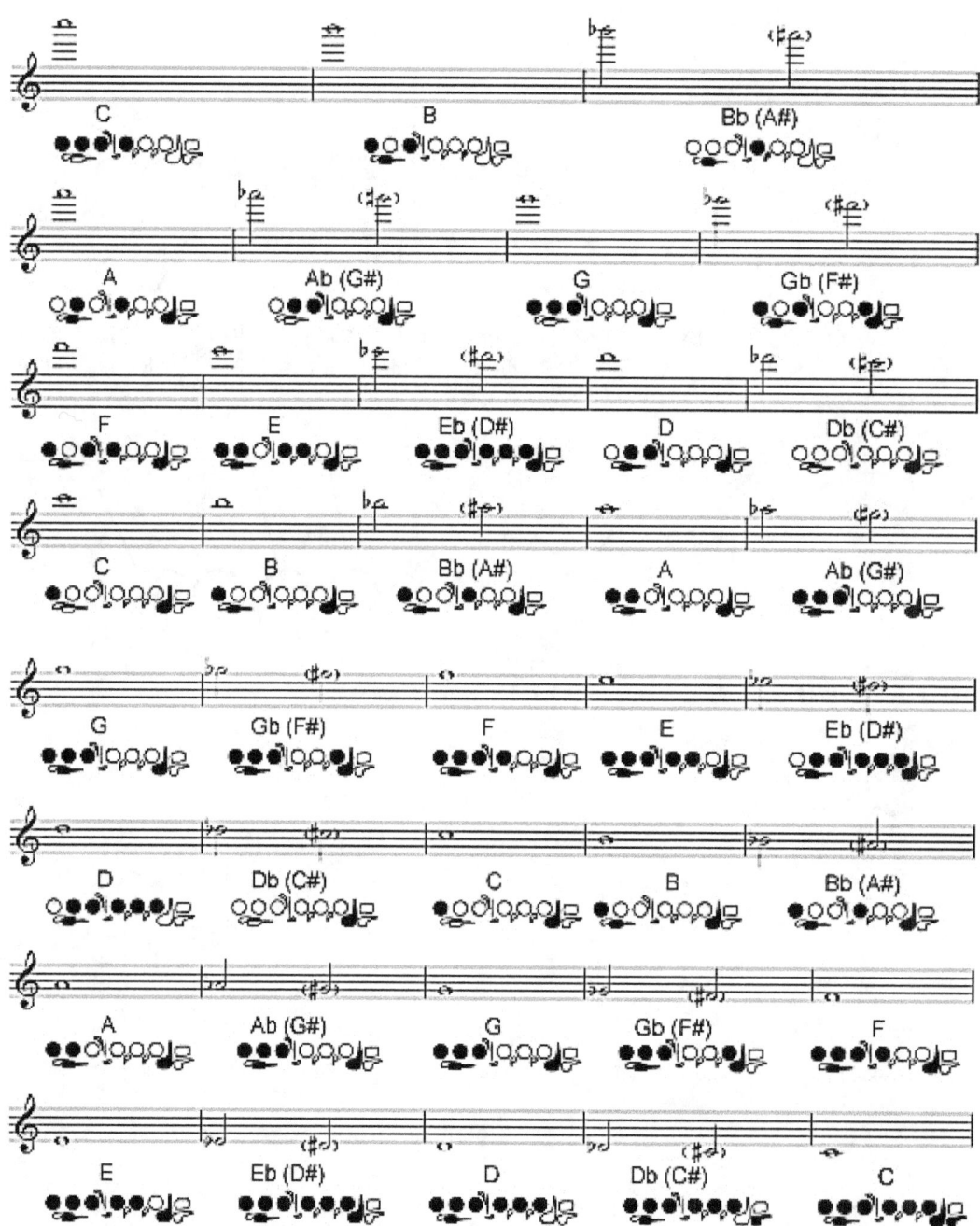

Chapter 3

What Are the Different Kinds of Flutes?

The Flute Family—The most popular flute family instruments are the piccolo and flutes, ranging from the concert flute in C to the bass flute in C.

Transposing Instruments—Some instruments are called transposing instruments and are referred to as being in a certain key. You will see an Eb soprano flute, an Eb saxophone, or an F horn. These key names refer to the actual note you will hear when the written note C is played on the instrument.

A Review of Transposition—You must understand transposition to determine the exact sound your instrument produces from a written note. A non-transposing instrument will sound as written. The written note C will sound like C. When the written note C is played on a transposing instrument, the note sounded will be the note in the instrument's name. When playing a written C, a transposing instrument such as a Bb clarinet will sound a Bb. To increase the range of an instrument, other versions of the same instrument are made in different sizes. Smaller sizes produce notes in higher ranges, and larger sizes produce notes in lower ranges. This arrangement allows you to play these different instruments using the same fingering. The result is these become transposing instruments.

The four members of the flute family now in use are:

The concert flute in C which is probably the one you are playing and is used in orchestral, concert band, marching band music, and solo works.

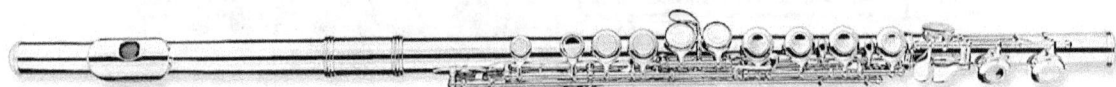

11

The piccolo in C is a small C flute sounding one octave higher than the concert flute.

The alto flute in G sounds a fourth lower than the written note.

Two Models of the bass flute in C sound an octave lower than the written note.

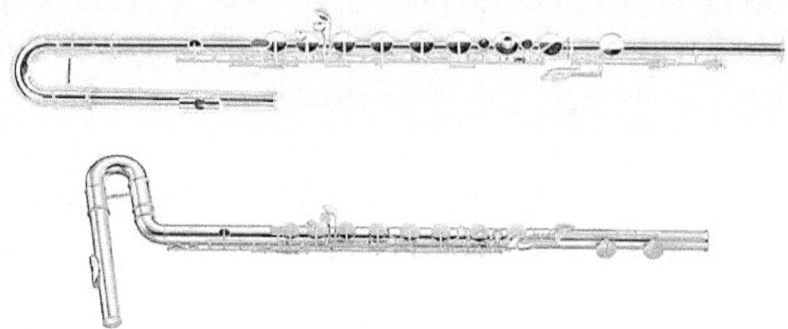

Other flutes used for special effects are:

The treble flute in G

the soprano in Eb

the tenor in Bb

the contrabass flute in C   the double contrabass flute in C

The contrabass flute sounds two octaves below the written note, and the double contrabass three octaves below the written note. Their music is written in the treble clef.

Modified Flutes—There are ways to change a flute to accommodate the needs of the handicapped and small children who are not physically mature enough to reach all the keys.

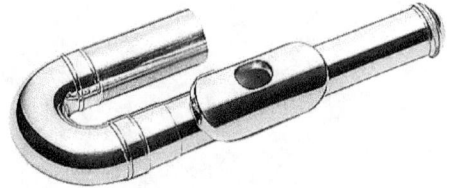

A curved U-shaped head joint can be used to shorten the distance between the embouchure hole and the first key on the instrument's body. Several manufacturers

make a curved head joint, and it can often be used on different flute brands.

Another option is the Wave-Line head joint with a U-shaped dip in its center rather than having the entire head joint in a U shape.

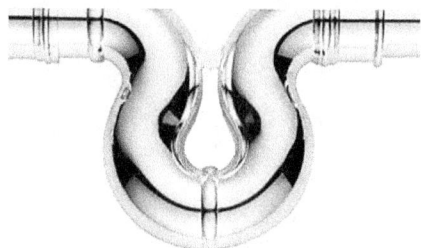

The manufacturer claims this shape distributes the weight evenly throughout the instrument. This head joint also shortens the distance between the embouchure hole and the first key.

There are flutes designed with deep key pad cups and depressions in the plateau keys that help those with difficulty fingering the instrument. With this design, the player has a better feel of the keys.

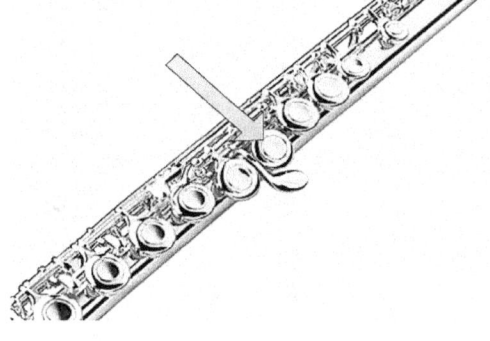

Deep Key Pad Cups

Flute plugs can be put into the open holes for players with an open hole flute but have temporary difficulty covering the open key holes completely. These can remain in place until the player can cover the holes without assistance. The plugs are then easily removed.

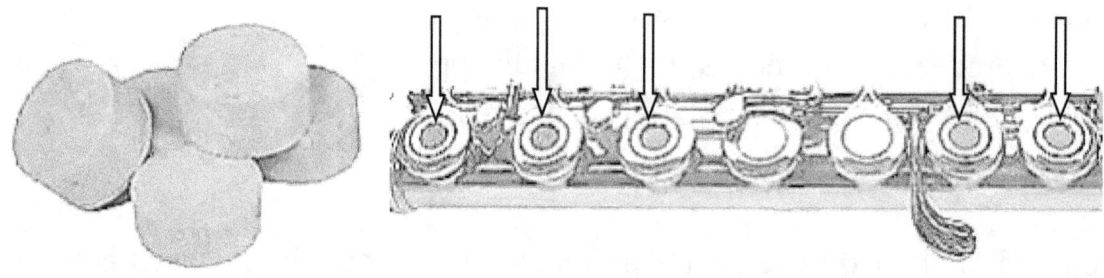

Flute Plugs

Different Lip Plates—The lip plate or embouchure plate supports your lower lip when in a playing position. Lip plates come in either straight or curved shapes.

Straight and Curved Lip Plates

The straight shape is more common and can produce a clear, flowing tone. The curved shape provides greater volume with less effort. With the curved design, your lips and chin are positioned closer to the embouchure hole, allowing greater tone production with less effort.

Different Embouchure Holes— The embouchure hole in the lip plate can be different shapes. Rectangular-shaped holes tend to produce a more forceful tone. Oval-shaped holes produce a mellow tone in the upper register. Round holes tend to produce a more balanced sound. As you advance in your studies, find a music dealer with a large flute inventory and try the different shaped embouchure holes to see how each reacts to your embouchure.

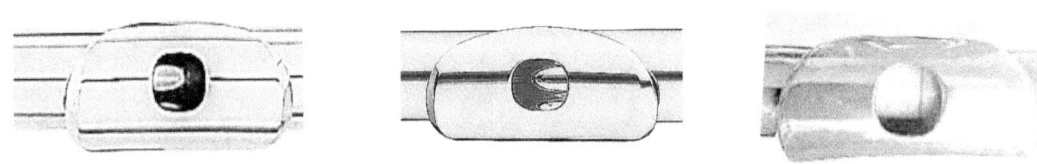

Different Shaped Embouchure Holes

Summary—The information above introduces some of the many different flutes in daily use and some not so often used. As you progress in your studies, spend some time learning more about these other instruments and, if possible, try to play some of them to see if you might want to add another instrument to your playing skills.

NOTES

Chapter 4

How Are Flutes Made?

Flutes can be made of different materials and with different head joints and key systems.

Head Joint—Beginning with the head joint, a solid steel bar is put into a machine press, forming a hollow tube slightly smaller on one end than the other (tapered) for the head joint.

Forming a Flute Head Joint

Another tube is used to make the flute's body. Small holes called pilot holes are drilled into the tube as the first step in creating tone holes.

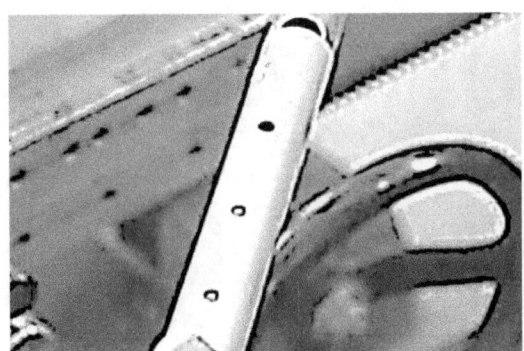 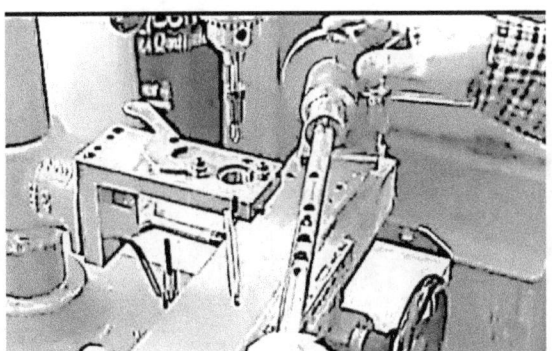

Drilling Tone Holes in a Flute Body

Tone Hole—A flute tone hole can be made separately from the body and then soldered in place, or it can be drawn from the material of the body itself.

To install separately made tone holes, spider-shaped markers made of a hard metal called titanium are placed in the pilot holes to support the placement of the tone holes. One tone hole will be placed around each spider, tied with copper wire, and then soldered in place.

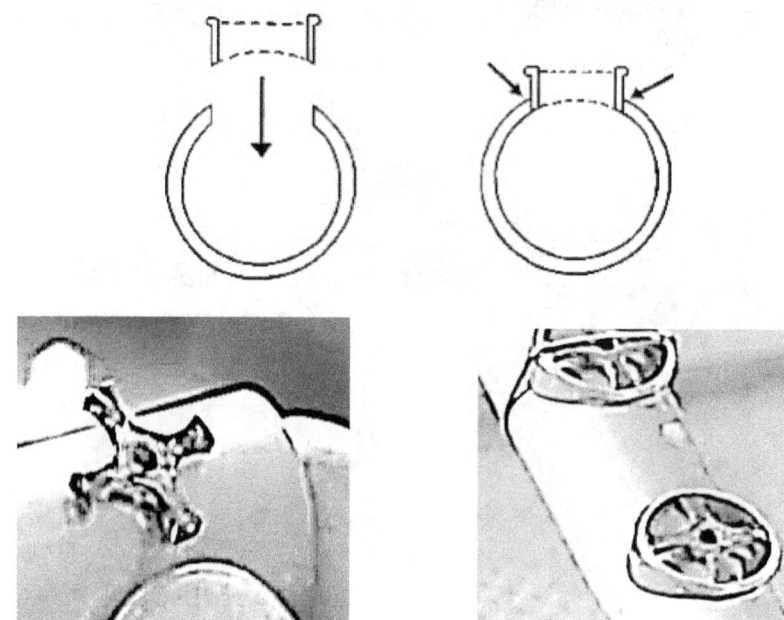

Positioning Separate Tone Holes Held with Copper Wire

A device called a profile cutter is then used to cut the tone holes in the body.

Profile Cutter Forming Tone Holes   **Finished Soldered Tone Hole**

Drawn Tone Holes—To make drawn tone holes, pilot holes are drilled in the flute's body. A series of highly polished metal drawing balls of gradually increasing sizes are pulled from the inside of the flute through the pilot hole. The balls pull the material from the body upward, forming a cup-like opening in the body. The edge of the opening is leveled and rolled to a smooth surface on which the pad can rest.

Drawn Tone Hole

Posts—Posts that hold the flute keys in place can be soldered directly onto the flute's body or onto a strip of metal called a rib. The rib can then be soldered onto the flute's body. The pictures below show posts being soldered onto a rib and the rib in place, ready to be soldered onto the flute's body.

 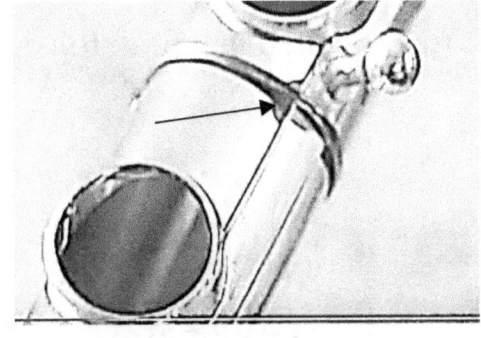

Soldering Posts onto a Rib **Rib onto a Body**

Keys—Making flute keys begins with creating a form for each key. Wax is poured into the form to make a wax mold of the key.

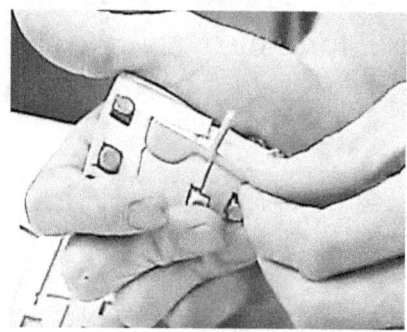

Wax Mold of a Flute Key

The wax key-shaped molds are removed from the form and assembled on a tree like the one pictured below.

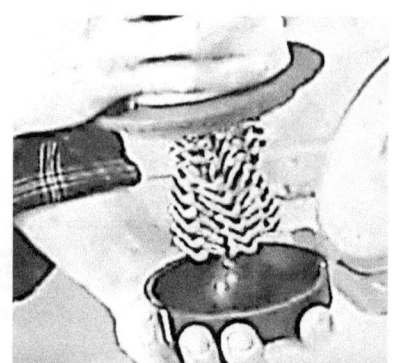

Key Tree

The tree is placed in a flask filled with plaster that will harden around the tree.

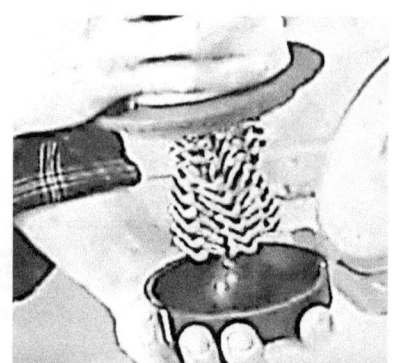
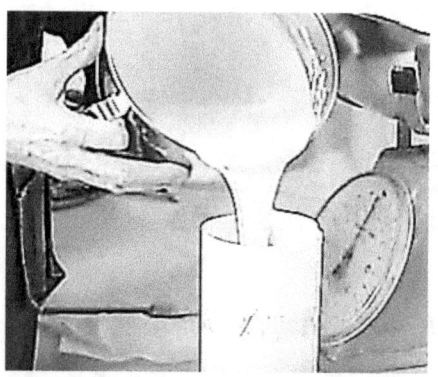

Preparing a Mold for a Wax Key Tree

After the plaster has hardened around the tree, the wax is melted, and a plaster cast is filled with the molten material used to make the keys. When cooled, the mold is removed, and a tree of metal keys remains. The new key parts are snipped off the tree and soldered together.

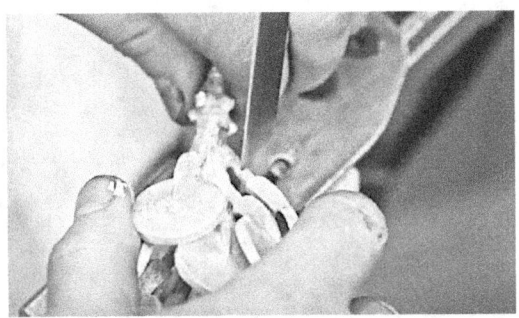

Snipping the Keys off the Tree

For hand-forged keys, the metal of choice, usually nickel silver, is used to shape individual parts of the key.

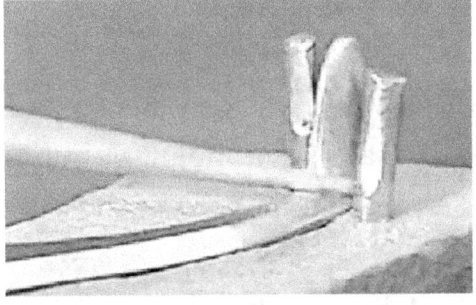

Hand Forged Keys

The parts are soldered together to form a complete key.

 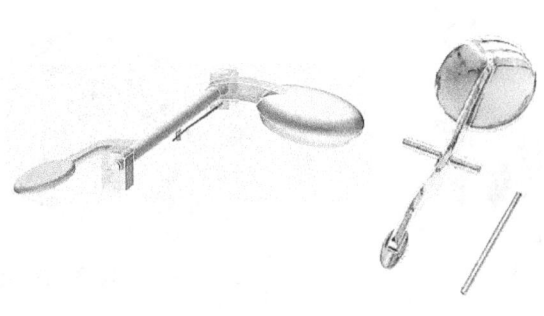

Soldering Flute Keys   **Complete Keys**

The keys are polished in preparation for assembly on the instrument.

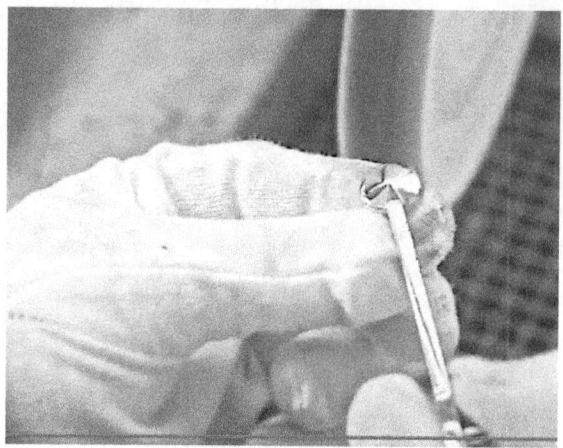

Polishing Keys

Installing Pads—Pads that cover the tone holes on a flute can be installed with a screw and washer system or by gluing them in place.

For the screw and washer system, a washer called a pad shim is placed in the pad cup, followed by a pad held in place by a metal washer and screw. Pad shims are used to be sure the pad will sit on the tone hole firmly without leaking.

In the first picture below, looking from left to right, you will see a washer and screw. Next is a pad, a pad cup with a shim/washer in it, a pad, a screw, and a metal cap that will hold it all together. The last picture shows a pad installed in a cup using the screw and washer system.

Screw and Washer Key Pad System

To glue a pad in a key pad cup, the craftsperson places special glue or lacquer in the cup and puts the pad in place.

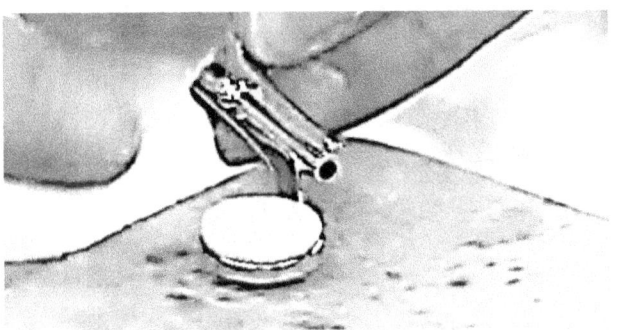

Pad Glued in Key Pad Cup

When all the key pads have been installed, the keys are put in place on the flute, the pads are checked for proper contact (seated) with the tone hole to prevent leaks, the flute is tested and adjusted, and the instrument is ready to go.

NOTES

Chapter 5

How Do I Take Care of My Flute?

Before you begin to learn about caring for your flute, let's spend a few moments reviewing how to put the parts together in a way that will not damage them.

1. Hold the body at the point closest to the head joint above the keys and gently twist the head joined into the body so the embouchure hole is in line with the nearest key.

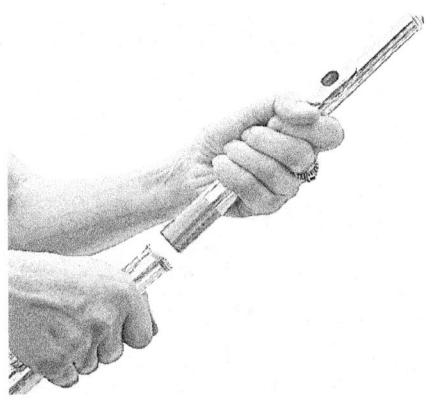

2. Holding the body at the point above the keys and the foot joint below the last key, gently twist the foot joint onto the body with the key rod (not the key) centered on the lowest key on the body.

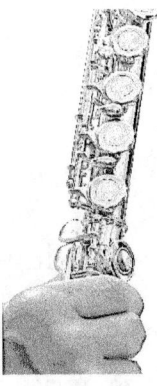

Flutes require "per use" care and more extensive periodic care. The per-use care includes cleaning, swabbing the head joint and bore, and making minor adjustments. Keeping a flute bore swabbed and cleaned after each use is essential to its well-being. Periodic care includes any major action or repair, such as complete cleaning, cleaning the bore, and lubricating moving key parts.

The Head Joint

Per Use—After each playing session, take apart your flute and clean the head joint bore with an appropriate swab. There are many swabs available, which will be discussed in chapter 8. You must choose the swab that suits you best, made for your flute. Wipe the embouchure plate with an alcohol wipe. These can be found in any drugstore.

Periodic Care for the Head Joint—Your flute head joint can be washed with mild soap and warm water. Before you begin this process, review the parts of the crown assembly described in chapter 1. Beginning from the left side, there is a crown (A), screw (B), first metal plate (C), cork (D), and second metal plate (E). Combined, they are called the crown assembly.

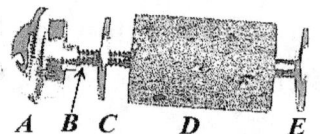 

Now, use the picture above as your guide:

1. Begin by removing the crown assembly.

   A. Remove the crown by turning it counterclockwise.

   B. Using your cleaning rod, push the crown assembly cork in toward the embouchure hole until the cork is out of the head joint.

   C. Using a clean cloth moistened with rubbing alcohol, wipe the cork clean.

   D. Apply a small amount of cork grease to the cork.

Now, continue cleaning the head joint.

2. Use a flute cleaning brush to gently scrub the head joint bore until it is perfectly clean.

3. Be sure to rinse the inside and outside of the head joint.

4. Dry the head joint thoroughly with a soft towel.

5. To disinfect your flute's head joint, use products specially designed for musical instrument mouthpieces. You can find these disinfectants in most music stores. Follow the directions on the package.

Now, let's replace the crown assembly.

1. Place the cork assembly into the head joint, ensuring the first plate goes in first.

2. You learned how to adjust the crown assembly in chapter 2.

3. For your convenience, here is a repeat of that process.

The crown assembly can move in or out and is used to tune your flute. Look carefully at the non-slotted end of your cleaning rod, and you will see a mark near the end of the rod. This mark is a guide to help you tune your flute.

After returning the crown assembly, place the tuning rod in the head joint so the mark on the tuning rod is visible through the embouchure hole. The crown assembly is in place when that mark is in the center of the embouchure hole.

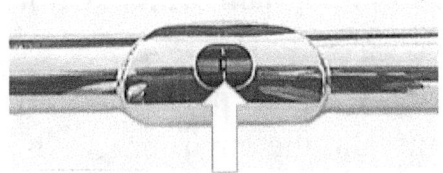

4. Replace the crown screw, and the job is done. Ask your teacher to help with tuning the first time you do it.

Bore Care

Per Use—Take apart your flute and clean the bore with an appropriate swab after each use. There are many swabs available, which will be discussed in chapter 8. You must choose the swab that suits you best, made for your flute.

Periodic Care—Choose a soft cloth that is long enough to wrap around the entire length of your tuning rod.

1. Dampen, but do not soak that cloth with isopropyl alcohol.
2. Insert the alcohol-damped cloth into the open slot at the end of your tuning rod and run the rod through the flute's bore using a twisting and in-and-out motion.
3. Repeat the process for the head and foot joints.

Key Maintenance

Per Use—The keys on flutes require several kinds of care. The parts that come into contact with your fingers should be wiped clean regularly to be determined by your hand hygiene. This is best done with a soft cloth or, for silver-plated keys, with a chemically treated silver polishing cloth. Under no circumstances should any liquid polish be used on keys. It is unnecessary, can harm the keys' motion, and might damage the pads. A wipe with your cloth of choice will do the job.

Periodically—Using a soft-bristle brush, such as those used for makeup, and brush off the lint and residue that may collect between the keys. If there is any evidence of a substance that the brush will not remove, use a Q-tip to take care of that. Be careful not to displace a spring or damage a pad during this process.

The next issue of importance in key maintenance is lubrication. Depending on use, the age of the instrument, and the environment in which it lives, make a judgment as to how often lubrication is needed, but be flexible since conditions such as climate, use, and locations may change during different periods throughout the year. Common sense without rigidity in decision-making is always the best route to take.

Selecting Key Oil

1. Avoid the more exotic concoctions. Try to identify the commercial oil with the best user rating and go with that.

2. If you are a flute oil wonk and are inclined to "study the market," you will find opinions such as avoiding light oil and being sure to use light oil.

3. This contradiction exists because light oil evaporates more quickly than oils of a greater viscosity (thickness). If you believe in oiling at every use, don't. Light oil tends to travel down the post to the instrument's body. This is messy and will collect dust and lint.

4. Some flute players feel that using thicker oils such as automobile gear, motor oil, or mineral oil is a better choice.

To test the oil's viscosity (thickness), turn the bottle up and down to see how the contents move. The slower the oil moves about, the thicker it is. When you have decided which oils should be considered, place a drop of each, side by side, on one end of a smooth, flat surface. Then, raise that end of the surface and observe the rate of speed at which the oils travel downward. Thicker oils will move more slowly.

With several choices, try each on one key using a different key for each trial. Do not combine different oils during the trial. Some brands will offer oils in different viscosities appropriate for different instruments. Be sure to use flute key oil.

The Process—There are many opinions (surprise) on how to apply oil to flute keys. Some suggestions are:

1. Use a drop of oil on the tip of a toothpick.

2. The use of an eyedropper (a bad idea because one drop may be too much oil).

3. Use a hypodermic needle or some other small pointed object to move the oil from the bottle to the key.

If you look at a key that is joined to the instrument, you will easily see where that drop of oil should be placed. Keys are held on a flute's body by posts through which a pivot screw is inserted to hold the key in place. These screws are connected to the key barrel, a tube on which a pivot screw secures the key from both sides.

In the picture below, the arrows point to an example of where a key is joined to the instrument. There are many more of these oiling places on your flute. At these points, you should put a drop of key oil.

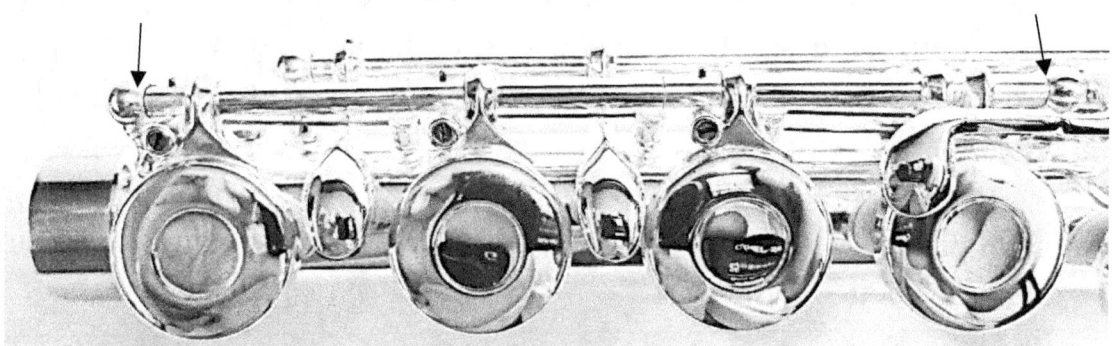

Flute Oiling Points

I recommend you use one of the oil brands that offer an application tip. This oil bottle with an appropriate-sized injection-type needle will dole out the amount needed for an application.

Key oil is needed to prevent rust, quiet the key's action, and lubricate the key's moving parts. To ensure that the oil you use on the keys does not seep onto the instrument's body, I recommend synthetic oil instead of petroleum-based. Synthetic oils are less likely to evaporate. Trial and error on your part will eventually allow you to pick a brand that will serve your needs. In the most general sense, you should apply oil sparingly as needed to all moving key parts.

The actual application of oil is a simple process. "Less is more." The amount of oil and how often it should be used should be minimal. Use the applicator tip to apply the smallest amount of oil possible to both sides of the key barrel at every point where a key that moves is connected to the instrument's posts. Work the key up and down to help the oil travel into the barrel. Decide how often it is necessary to do this depending on your circumstances and be flexible about that timing decision, should the circumstance of your use of the instrument change.

You will need to take greater action if a key's operation is sluggish or won't move at all. If that is the case, you will need additional equipment and the time and patience to fix the problem.

If you have any mechanical ability, this will be an easy job. If you consider yourself to be a "call the man" type, by all means, bring the instrument to a certified repair person.

You will need a flat surface on which to work, an appropriate size flute screwdriver, a needle nose plyer, a large absorbent cloth, a smaller absorbent cloth, isopropyl alcohol, pipe cleaners, penetrating oil, and the key oil of choice. You will be working on the soft cloth spread on a flat surface. I find a bath towel is best.

1. Spread the towel out on a flat surface.

2. Place the instrument section to be worked on the towel.

3. Remove all the lint and dust accumulated within the key system using a soft bristle brush.

4. Put a drop of oil on both sides of the barrel of the problem key.

5. Work the key up and down until it moves more easily than it did previously.

6. Loosen and then retighten the screw.

Should the screw be rusted or bound in place, use a single drop of penetrating oil at the contact points. Let the penetrating oil remain for 15 minutes while you work the key up and down periodically. Make every effort not to get the penetrating oil on the instrument's body.

When you feel enough time has passed, try to <u>tighten</u> the screw the tiniest bit to break the bind. Then try again to loosen the screw. During this process, you must use a screwdriver that is a perfect fit for that screw slot to help prevent stripping the screw. If you cannot move the screw, bring it to a professional.

7. If you are removing a pivot screw, it should come out easily. If it is a rod screw after the thread clicks, indicating it is unscrewed, remove the screw with the needle nose plyer. The key will come out of place, but it is easy to replace after the screw is cleaned.

8. Clean the rod screw with alcohol on the small rag.

9. Pass an alcohol-moistened pipe cleaner through the key's barrel.

10. Pass an oil-moistened pipe cleaner through the key's barrel.

11. Return the key to its original position and replace the screw.

If you find rust on the key springs during this process, use a Q-tip to swab the affected spring with some oil.

Sticking Pads—The best solution to sticking pads is preventing them from happening. If you, as the player, avoid any food or drink other than water one hour before playing your instrument, the likelihood of your pads' sticking will greatly diminish.

When you eat or drink, other than water, your breath carries minute particles of food and vapors that contain anything in your mouth at the time, through your instrument and onto its pads. If you do not eat or drink, there is still some small chance of sticking pads caused by the moisture that the pads will inevitably pick up, combined with dust and residues of any kind in the environment.

Another cause of sticking pads can be any bore or key oil seepage that might migrate to the tone hole edges and then to the pads. To avoid this situation, you must follow the "less is more" rule when applying oil to your instrument.

Treatment—Before treating a sticking pad, be sure a weak spring is not the cause of the problem. Bending the spring slightly in the same direction it already takes can make a significant difference. If that does not help, proceed with the pad cleaning process.

Holding the instrument with the offending key located next to your ear, work the key. If the pad is sticky, you will hear a subtle clicking sound showing the pad sticking to the tone hole. If that sound is present, move on to treating the pad. There are several approaches to treating a sticking pad.

If the pad is old or showing signs of wear, the best solution is to remove the key, clean the tone hole edge with alcohol, and replace the pad with a new one.

If the pad is in good condition and the tone hole edge is clean, you might want to try some of the remedies on the market. There are various pad cleaning papers that you can place between the offending key and its tone hole. Place the paper between the key pad and the tone hole, gently close the key onto the paper, and withdraw it.

Another option is using key pad powders, which are supposed to remedy the sticky pad problem when applied to the pad.

Some technicians recommend swabbing the pad with a Q-tip moistened in lighter fluid. Others suggest the same process using isopropyl alcohol.

The opponents of these methods claim that the paper products will damage the pads, the powders will build up on the pad and worsen the problem, and the lighter fluid is dangerous and can dry out the pads. A sticky pad is not the end of the world. Over the years, I have used these procedures and found they all work depending on the severity of the condition. You will have to decide which to use by trial and error.

Summary—Flute maintenance is more labor-intensive than most instruments because of its numerous parts and mechanical complexity. You will find that the opinions on how these instruments should be maintained are numerous, in many cases contradictory, and at best not supported by convincing empirical evidence to which you can turn.

Your best direction would be to evaluate your situation in terms of your particular instrument's requirements, how often and where it is used, where and for how long it is stored without use, the climate in which you live, and whatever directions were included with the original packaging if the instrument was purchased new.

Trial and error in selecting the products will eventually bring you to suitable equipment and materials for your situation. As a rule, move thoughtfully, slowly, and intelligently and remember that less is more.

Chapter 6

How Should I Plan My Practice Sessions?

You have heard the old saying that "practice makes perfect." Well, practice can make perfect, but only if you practice with understanding, patience, and the will to "get it right."

Playing an exercise or musical selection often will make it better only if you understand how the piece should sound and know how to make it sound that way. Playing a piece incorrectly repeatedly can result in your learning to play it wrong well. Here are some suggestions that will help you get the best results from your practice period:

1. Select a place in your home where you can practice without disturbing your family and where their daily life will not distract you from your work.

2. Pick a practice time that comfortably fits your daily study schedule. Try to use that same time each day.

3. Set a long-term general goal. Then, set some short-term goals that will help you reach the long-term goal. Choose a topic like tone quality, intonation, phrasing, and dexterity (moving your fingers fast) as some of these short-term goals. Then, apply them to your long-term goal of making beautiful music.

4. Have a plan for each practice period. What part of your long-term goal do you want to accomplish in each period? For example, "Today, I will work on tone quality and embouchure."

5. How long and how often should you practice? Daily practice is best. However, how long you practice should vary with your short-term goal. Shorter daily practice periods produce better results than less frequent long sessions.

6. After you have set your goal and begun to practice, decide on the amount of time and how often you will need to practice to achieve each target.

7. Discuss your plans with your teacher, who can help you make the plan and reach your goal.

8. Equipment—You must have all the necessary equipment for a successful practice session. Your equipment should include a music stand, metronome, chair if you plan to sit, cleaning cloth, swab, and whatever else you need to be comfortable.

Breathing—Before you continue planning your practice sessions, let's think about your breath, which is the source of the sound you will be making on your flute.

A muscle that separates your lungs from your stomach area controls your normal breathing process. This muscle is called a diaphragm. As you breathe, your diaphragm moves up and down. When it moves down, it increases the area in your lung cavity, causing a vacuum that your lungs fill by drawing in air. When the diaphragm moves up, the lung cavity is smaller, and the air in your lungs is pushed out. You can see a great animated example of diaphragmatic breathing on Wikipedia. Search *diaphragmatic breathing* and look at the right-hand side of the first page for the diagram.

As a flute player, one of the most important skills you must master is controlling your diaphragm and, in so doing, controlling your airflow, which is the fuel supply for the tone you produce on your flute. Your diaphragm is regulated by your ABS (abdominal muscles). Expanding and contracting those muscles allows you to move your diaphragm up or down.

Try this! Lie down on a flat surface and relax. Place a book on your abdomen and breathe in and out. As you do so, you will notice that the book on your abdomen rises and falls as you breathe. When you breathe in, the book will rise; as you breathe out, the book will fall.

Now breathe out all the air in your lungs by contracting your ABS. Then take a deep breath in by expanding your ABS. Do not move any other body part, such as raising your shoulders or expanding your chest. Raising your shoulders does nothing; your chest will expand as your lungs fill with air. This conscious expansion and contraction of your abdominal muscles are called diaphragmatic breathing. It is something you do all day long without thinking about it.

To apply this procedure to play the flute, you must take a deep breath by expanding your diaphragm as much as possible. Remember not to expand your chest or raise your shoulders. Your lungs should be full of air. Now let the air out through pursed lips or play a long tone on your flute. As you run out of air, give an extra push on your ABS, and you will notice that there will still be a bit more air left to use. Practice this process regularly to develop breath control. The better you control your airflow through "conscious diaphragmatic breathing," the greater the fuel supply you will have for your embouchure.

The Process—Use the following ideas to make your practice period productive.

1. Warm up with some simple scales using long tones that start very softly (pianissimo—*ppp*), increase in volume (crescendo) to a full sound (forte—*fff*), and then gradually diminish the sound (diminuendo or dim.) back to the original *ppp*. Listen as you play. Are you playing in tune and with the best tone quality you can produce?

2. After warming up with some long tones, add your own rhythmic patterns to those same scales. Listen carefully to intonation as you play. Playing in tune is a must for any flutist.

3. As you advance you can expand the warmup material to include exercises.

4. Follow your warmup by playing a tune that you like. Enjoy the music.

5. Improvisation is fun. Make up a tune or try to play a tune "by ear." No need for printed music here.

6. Start practicing the material your teacher assigned in your last lesson. Follow the instructions carefully. Listen to yourself, sing the music before you play it, feel the rhythm, and be sure you are playing in tune.

7. Record yourself on your cell phone as you play. Then listen to the recording and be critical of your intonation, phrasing, and general musicianship.

8. Did you like what you heard? If your answer is yes—great! If it is not, think of what you did not like. Figure out how you can make it better. Then, make it better. Check again to be sure you are playing in tune, using proper embouchure and phrasing. Are you keeping a proper playing position?

Apps and Your Cell Phone—Using your cell phone or computer, you can search for "Apps for flute practice." You will find many that are free and will help you practice better. Some sites also have free music that you can print. Others show playing techniques and play-a-long sessions where you join others to play flute music. Use the same search on YouTube to find many sites you will enjoy watching while learning about playing and caring for your flute.

Summary—Developing a structure for your practice sessions that works for you will increase your level of achievement. Playing "stuff" without a plan may be fun but does not encourage learning. If you are building a brick wall, you must begin with a solid foundation on which that wall will rest. Your practice periods are the foundation upon which your performance will rest.

Chapter 7

A Survey of the History of Woodwind Instruments

The Flute—The flute you are now playing results from 43,000 years of history. It probably all began in Slovenia, a European country bordering Italy. In Slovenia, a cave bear's femur (thighbone) carved to look like a primitive flute with several tone holes was discovered. Another such instrument made from a vulture's wing bone was found in Germany. That instrument is estimated to be about 35,000 years old. These and other objects tell us that very early on, humankind was becoming aware that a stream of air passing through a tube could produce sound.

Simple flute-like instruments dating back to the pre-Christian era have been discovered in numerous countries. Instruments made from crane bones dated 9000 years old and others made of bamboo from 433 B.C. were discovered in China. Below are some examples of primitive wind instruments. Search Google Images Primitive Flutes to see many other examples.

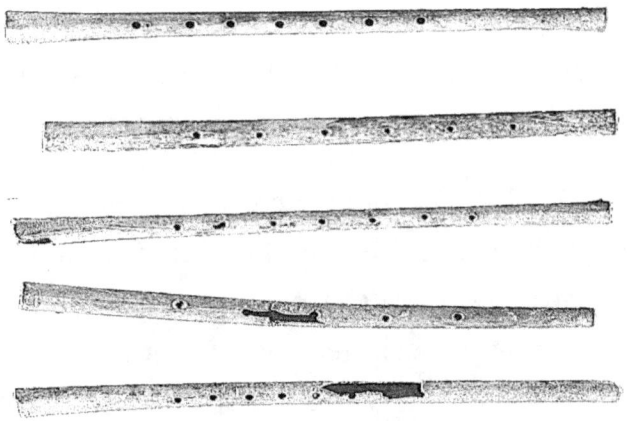

Below is a picture of today's modern flute. Quite a difference!

In 2004 in southern Germany, an instrument made from a mammoth tusk and two other similar instruments made from swan bones were discovered. Similar instruments have been found in many locations throughout the world. This tells us that there is no absolute way to assign an accurate time or location to the "invention" of the flute. We must be satisfied with the theory that the flute evolved along with the development of humankind.

By the sixteenth century, the flute had been developed into a one-piece cylinder with six tone holes. Covering the holes with the fingers allowed the player to produce different notes within a limited range. To make up for that limitation, the instruments were made in different sizes, producing different pitches. Larger instruments produced lower sounds, while smaller instruments produced higher sounds. That progress reached a point in the eighteenth century when flute makers began to develop key systems. As a result, we now enjoy the flute we are studying.

Jacques-Martin Hotteterre (1674–1763), renowned flutist and instrument maker of the time, is credited with improving the transverse flute by devising the three-piece design with a separate head joint, body, and foot joint structure. From that period on through the early eighteen-hundreds, improvements were made by relocating and resizing the six-tone holes and adding keys. This all resulted in improved intonation and a greater capability to perform chromatics.

Theobald Boehm (1794–1881), In the early 1800s, Boehm, a jeweler, and goldsmith, an accomplished flutist and flute maker, determined that larger, properly spaced tone holes would produce a better tone quality and improved intonation. For approximately twenty years, he redesigned the instrument producing a key system on a three-piece cylindrical body that, with modifications, became the instrument we know today.

The Following Is a Timeline for the Evolution of the Flute

1000–1400—The Medieval period in world history. The beginnings of society as we now know it.

Below is a reproduction of an instrument that was called a flute during the years 1000 through 1400. Look at the end of the instrument, and you will see no embouchure hole like the one on your flute. In its place is a cut in the wood, which makes a sharp edge (arrow) against which the air blown into the instrument strikes and produces a sound. This type of sound-maker is called a fipple.

Compare the fipple to the flute embouchure hole pictured below.

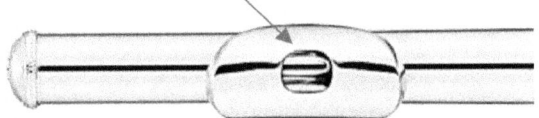

When you play your flute, you must direct a stream of air against the edge (arrow) of your flute's embouchure hole. In a fipple instrument, the air stream is directed for you to the exact spot. You might be familiar with a recorder instrument pictured below. A recorder is a fipple instrument.

The early instruments, called flutes, had no keys and six equally spaced tone holes. We now name these fipple instruments recorders.

1400–1600—The Renaissance Period in World History. A period of reawakening where society began to understand art, science, and music.

Adding an embouchure hole and spacing the tone holes in two sets of three was the next step in developing the flute you now play. These instruments had a better-sounding upper register but were still not great in the lower notes.

1600–1760—The Baroque Period in World History. A period when music, art, architecture, and the general style of living became very elaborate and highly crafted. Much music was written with several complicated, layered melodies at the same time. This is called counterpoint.

During these years, the flute was divided into four and then three sections. The bore (inside tube) was tapered, being larger at the embouchure hole and gradually getting smaller toward the end. With these adjustments, the flute sound improved and could be tuned.

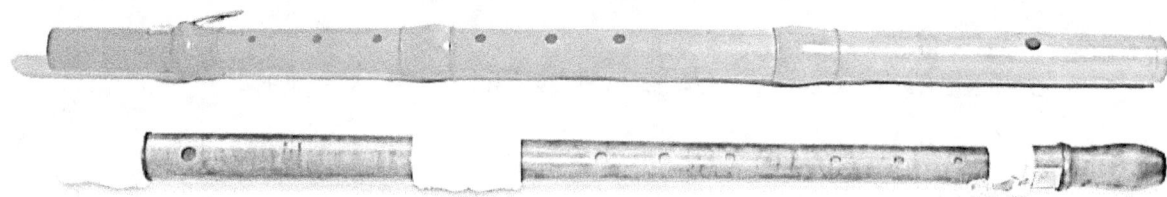

1760–1820—The Classical Period in World History. A period when music and the arts became simpler and music was written with a single melody and harmony (chords). The flute becomes a part of the orchestra with music by Haydn, Mozart, and Beethoven.

George Catlin (1778–1852), a musical instrument maker, made a variety of experimental flutes beginning with one key and gradually adding keys. These additional keys improved the intonation of the instruments and made it possible for a flute player to play more notes with greater ease.

Rick Wilson's Historical Flute Page http://www.oldflutes.com/boehm.htm is a great source of information on the flute's history. Below is a picture of two early Boehm flutes from Rick Wilson's website.

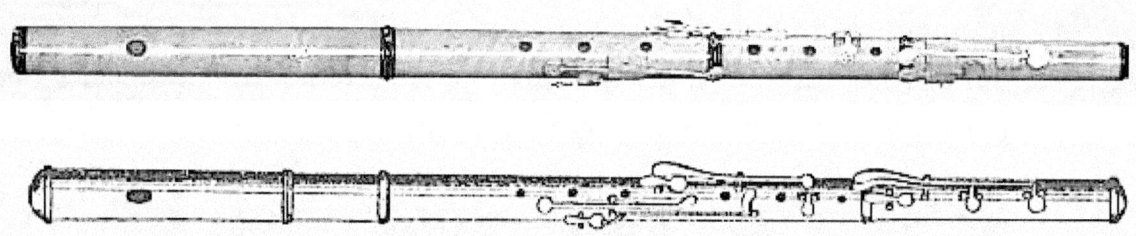

Rick Wilson indicates that these photos and essays may be copied for personal use or used in moderation on web pages, etc., as long as he is clearly acknowledged as the source. All but minimal use of the photos or essays on the web should be accompanied by a link to these pages.

The following is a survey of the history of the other most popular woodwind instruments now in use: the clarinet, saxophone, oboe, and bassoon. You will read about instruments that preceded those, some by several thousand years. Other instruments invented at a known time in music history will receive a more accurate account of their development.

The aulos is perhaps the flute-like instrument most frequently represented in ancient Greek illustrations, literature, and the Bible. Dating as far back as the sixth century B.C., the aulos was used as an accompaniment to vocal performers and as a solo instrument. The primary settings for their use extended to festive occasions of all kinds, athletic events, and funerals. Originally made of various kinds of wood, such as cane or boxwood, more sophisticated bronze, bone, and ivory models appeared.

One version of the aulos was constructed with two pipes, each with a double reed as its sound generator. Different illustrations show the instrument as two units held individually while being played simultaneously. Variations of the aulos will have five to seven tone holes on each pipe, and more advanced models with a ring-type device at the top of the pipes. This was used to alter the pitch.

In 1921, twenty-three feet of tubing and assorted fragments were discovered in the tomb of Queen Amanishakheto in Meroe, Sudan. These are believed to be sections of different types of auloi that were parts of a professional musician's equipment.

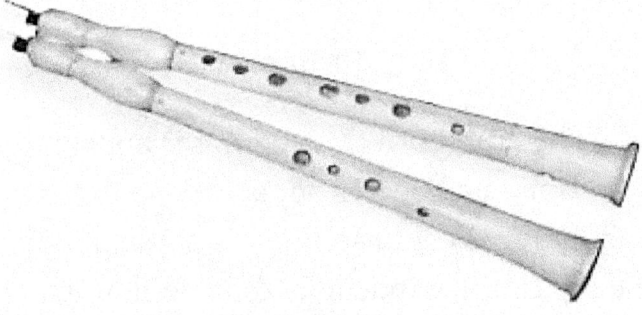

Aulos

Windcap Instruments

Using a windcap instrument, the player blew through a hole in the top of the windcap and, in so doing, activated the double reed inside. The disadvantage of a windcap sound generator is the player's lack of control over the action of the reed other than to start, increase, or decrease volume to some degree and to stop the sound. All the nuances of pitch, volume, and timbre associated with a player's contact with a reed are lost in a windcap instrument.

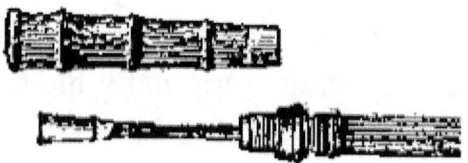

Windcap

The Zummara—The zummara, native to Egypt, had a windcap sound generator. The instrument had two pipes, one functioning as a drone supplying a continuous underlying tone. The other pipe was used to play the melody. The player was required to finger both pipes by spanning the holes on each pipe simultaneously. The intonation was dreadful.

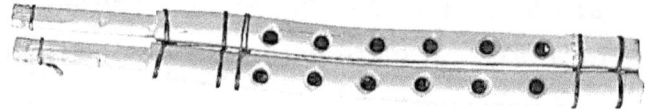

Zummara

The Crumhorn—The crumhorn (curved horn) appeared in Germany in the late fourteenth century and maintained its popularity in Germany, Italy, and the surrounding areas for about three centuries. As a windcap instrument, the player blew through a hole in the top of the windcap and, in so doing, activated the double reed inside.

The crumhorn was constructed with a cylindrical bore similar to a clarinet. This resulted in the instrument's overblowing (raising the register) at the twelfth instead of an octave at which a conical bore instrument would sound. The crumhorn had fingering like the clarinet's chalumeau (lowest) register but was limited to about an octave. The instrument was difficult to play in the upper range, had a somewhat raucous sound, and did not excel in pitch accuracy. Below is a picture of a crumhorn and a breakdown of its windcap reed unit.

Crumhorn

Single Reed Instruments

Single-reed instruments of the idioglot version, where the reed is carved from part of the instrument, date back to three thousand B.C.

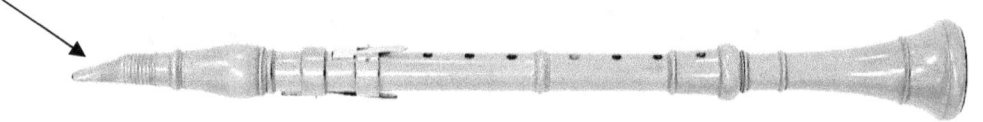

We might speculate that these instruments were the precursors of the clarinet and saxophone.

The Chalumeau—Chalumeau (chalumeaux plural) was used throughout central Europe as early as the twelfth century. The early chalumeau lacked musical sophistication in intonation and tone quality, so its use and repertoire were relegated to folk rather than classical compositions. Eventually, improvements were made to the instrument so that by 1700, the chalumeau evolved into a single reed woodwind instrument with seven tone holes, one key on the front, and one hole on the back. Its range, from F3 below middle C to A4 above middle C, was equal to that of the present-day clarinet's lower so-called chalumeau register. This more sophisticated chalumeau gained acceptance throughout France and Germany and became part of the popular instrumentation.

Chalumeau

Because the chalumeau had a range of only twelve notes, the players were required to use as many as four different models to cover the range from F3, a fifth below middle C, to Bb5 above the treble staff. At this time, eight original chalumeaux are in existence. These are models for contemporary makers who produce chalumeaux to satisfy the present market.

The Clarinet

John Christoph Denner (1655–1707), an instrument maker, along with his son Jacob, is credited with advancing the technology of the chalumeau by first adding two keys and then gradually changing the size of the tone holes to improve intonation. Denner then relocated and added keys and a bell, increasing the length of the instrument. The result was a clarinet with an extended range to include the higher (clarion) register.

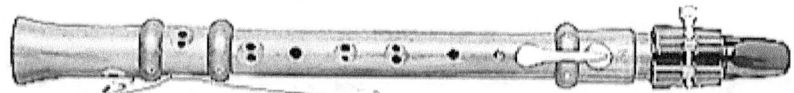

Early Clarinet

In the Middle Ages, the word clarion was applied to the trumpet. Because notes played on the clarinet in the upper register paralleled the intensity of those of a trumpet, the term was applied to that clarinet register. Combined with the chalumeau or lower register and eventually extending the range up to the altissimo, higher register, by 1800, the clarinet became the single reed instrument of choice, relegating the chalumeau instrument to a lesser status.

From then on, a series of artist/instrument makers modified the instrument over 300 years to the point where it is now the contemporary clarinet. During that period, Ivan Muller, Hyacinthe Klosé, Auguste Buffet, Theobald Boehm, Heinrich Joseph Baermann, Eugène Albert, and Adolphe Sax each contributed modifications that would result in the contemporary clarinet with a key system consisting of 17 to 22 keys and 4 to 6 ring keys.

Ivan Müller (1786–1854) invented the air-tight pad, making possible the addition of enough keys to facilitate playing chromatics on the clarinet. Müller pads replaced the flat brass keys with leather pads that did not cover the tone holes. Müller also invented the metal ligature, which replaced the string or wire used up to that point to secure the reed to the mouthpiece. An interesting note is that, to date, some clarinetists still prefer the use of string in place of a ligature.

In addition to inventing the air-tight pad and the ligature, Müller redesigned the clarinet to contain thirteen keys to service redesigned tone holes. The result was a greater facility for the player and improved intonation. Müller's system had no ring keys.

Müller System Clarinet

Eugene Albert (1816–1890) was a Belgian clarinet maker who developed a key system based on the Müller 13 key system but with the addition of two ring keys. Adolphe Sax, a clarinet maker and saxophone inventor, was Albert's tutor. Sax was responsible for adding the two ring keys to Albert's key system. After that, Albert added two rings, resulting in the "Albert System" with thirteen keys and four ring keys. This arrangement enhanced the intonation of the clarinet and once again made fingering and cross-fingering easier.

Albert's clarinets were very well received because of their excellent craftsmanship and intonation; however, there was one limitation. The instruments were made to pitch A=452 vibrations per second, meaning that the general intonation was higher than the standard A=440. Albert's son, also a clarinet maker, seeing his father's instruments going out of favor, built a clarinet to tune to A=440, extending the popularity of the Albert System clarinets into the twentieth century.

Albert System Clarinet

Hyacinthe Klosé (1808–1880), August Buffet (1789–1864), and the Boehm System—The Boehm key system, originally invented by Theobold Boehm for the flute, served as a model for Hyacinthe Klosé and August Buffet to create a key system for the clarinet. Over about four years, starting in 1839, they modified ring keys and side keys, enabling clarinetists to play chromatics and difficult passages with comparative ease and a much-improved intonation. Theobold Boehm had no part in this transition except to have been the inspiration for what is called the Boehm clarinet key system. In the last quarter of the nineteenth century, Buffet introduced the full Boehm system, which was accepted worldwide and replaced the Albert System.

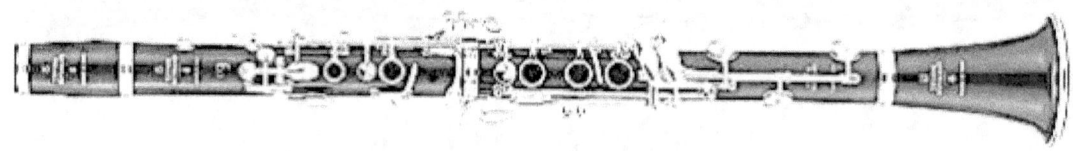

Boehm System Clarinet

Oskar Öhler (1858–1936) As clarinet technology developed to a point where a player could perform at a high level technically, a need grew to improve intonation and tone quality further. Öhler achieved this by repositioning the tone holes, modifying the fingering, and adding keys up to twenty-eight. He also reduced the diameter of the bore, extended its length, and decreased the diameter of the mouthpiece bore. Öhler's concepts for tone improvement were carried on by his students and eventually into the late twentieth century by the Wurlitzer Manufacturing Company, whose clarinets are most popular in Germany.

Öhler System Clarinet

The Saxophone

The Saxophone—The saxophone can be considered the first woodwind instrument invented instead of being an offshoot of some instrument from the past. Adolph Sax (1814-1894), born in Belgium, was a flutist, clarinetist, and instrument maker who received recognition for improving the timbre and key system and extending the lower range of the bass clarinet. He was also noted for making the ophicleide, a brass instrument played with a cup mouthpiece with tone holes fitted with as many as twelve woodwind-like padded keys.

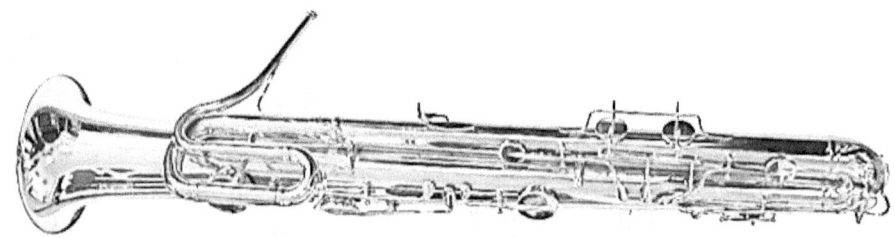

Ophicleide

With this background, we might guess that the stage was set in Sax's mind for a single reed woodwind instrument that would produce the sound characteristics of a brass instrument. Sax also intended to design an instrument to overblow at the octave rather than the twelfth, as does the clarinet to simplify the fingering. And so appeared the saxophone.

Sax designed and built a series of 14 saxophones spanning the tonal range from sopranino to contrabass. In 1846, he was granted a patent on these instruments, making him among the first instrument makers to design, build, and produce a woodwind instrument rather than evolving from a series of previous such instruments.

After the patent expired, several other makers improved the saxophone, enhanced the key system to facilitate playing legato passages and chromatics, changed the bell, and extended the instrument's range to F6. Modifying the key work replaced two octave keys that operated the two octave vents with one key to control both vents. The saxophone now holds an important position in all categories of instrumental music.

Below is a picture of the complete line of saxophones produced by the Selmer Musical Instrument Manufacturing Company. From left to right, they are the Eb Sopranino, Bb Soprano, Eb Alto, Bb Tenor, Eb Baritone, Bb Bass, and Eb Contrabass saxophones.

Saxophone Family Instruments

Saxophone Mouthpiece History

Progress in the study of the technology of musical instruments shows that an instrument's source of sound, namely the mouthpiece/reed, is primarily responsible for the quality of that sound. The mouthpiece is the major contributing factor to the quality of the tone produced. The saxophone's mouthpiece has proven to be an extreme example of this position. Saxophonists should select it carefully and consider their aptitude, physical characteristics, embouchure, and playing experience.

Many changes have taken place in the design of the saxophone's mouthpiece since the original was made in 1840. It has been lengthened, shortened, enlarged, made smaller, cored out, tapered, colored, and re-shaped using every sort of material conceivable. Each of these changes has contributed to the many opinions of the sound of the saxophone since each change in mouthpiece design resulted in a change in tone quality or timbre.

The sound generator (mouthpiece reed combination) is almost entirely responsible for the quality and timbre of the saxophone. The early alto saxophone mouthpiece had a tube-shaped bore with no taper. The throat was round, and the tone chamber had a bulbous portion preceding the window. The wall surfaces were concave, giving it a tone that was mellow and lacked the edge often associated with the saxophone.

The 1930s saw the era of the large dance band, which demanded a sound that would be better matched with brass instruments. At that time, the woodwind and brass instruments were distributed equally in these bands. It became necessary to strengthen the sound of the reeds to match that of the brasses.

Since sophisticated devices for sound evaluation were not yet available, those involved in research and development needed to rely on instinct to find remedies. They experimented with materials of various densities and expansion measurements and redesigned the structure of the mouthpiece interior. This experimentation produced many unsatisfactory mouthpieces that led to the decline of the reputation of the saxophone as a serious instrument.

During that time, one mouthpiece was developed, which modified the original and helped the saxophone regain some of its original popularity. The new model mouthpiece produced a richer tone, emphasizing the upper notes. Following that, the industry developed another design modeled on the shape of the clarinet mouthpiece. This mouthpiece produced an extraordinarily powerful and penetrating sound, and it gained favor from dance band music performers who competed with their brass-playing counterparts. Simultaneously, classical musicians stopped using the saxophone due to the instrument's increasing incompatibility with symphonic sounds.

Further experimentation with more advanced technological sound-evaluating devices led to smaller chambers, which proved unsatisfactory, and then to the double-tone chamber, which had a tapered cylindrical bore and a smaller tone chamber and throat. This mouthpiece produced a very aggressive sound, enabling a player to blast out the notes but creating a greater likelihood that the less experienced player might lose control of tone quality and intonation.

A mouthpiece that seemed to strike a suitable balance, including most of the above features, produced a tone acceptable to most "classical" musicians. Having a round chamber, it produced a smooth, mellow tone yet with a bright edge. The diagram shows the parts of a present-day saxophone mouthpiece.

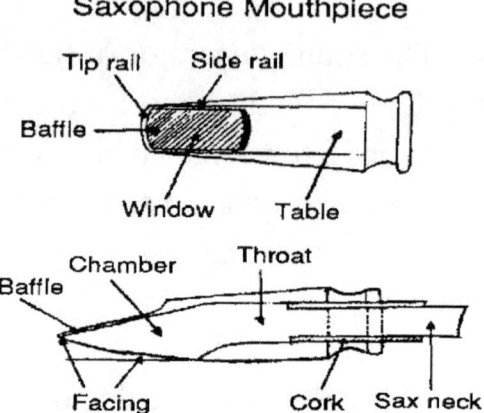

Double Reed Instruments

The Oboe

The Shawm—Dating back to the twelfth century, the Shawm was a double reed, conical bore instrument with eight tone holes, seven on the front and one on the back. The reed on some ancient shawms was surrounded by a windcap called a pirouette. With this device in place, the player's lips had no direct contact with the reed, making it possible to play the instrument while on horseback or marching.

As stated above, the disadvantage of this arrangement was the player's lack of control of intonation, expression, and nuanced volume normally afforded by direct contact with the reed. The resulting sound was piercing and very rich in overtones. See page 71 for more on overtones. Its strident tone was intended to compete with and accompany trumpets and percussion instruments.

As the Shawm evolved, the tone quality was somewhat modified by a change in its architecture. The range was increased by an octave, and the bore and tone holes were reduced in size. Various-sized shawms were made to cover the range from soprano to bass, the latter being less than successful due to their inconvenient size. The

Shawm enjoyed popularity up to the middle of the seventeenth century when the oboe began to make its presence known.

The Oboe—The oboe is a derivative of the Shawm but with a more advanced key system that permits the player to perform with reasonable ease. Removing the windcap gives the player direct contact with the double reed, improving intonation, timbre, and volume control. The result is an instrument compatible with a modern orchestra instead of the Shawm, which produces a more "independent" sound.

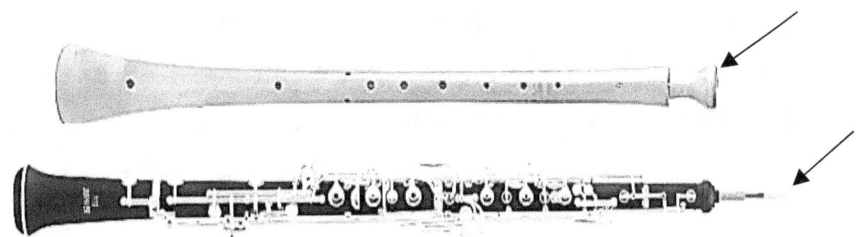

Shawm and Oboe

The oboe body was divided into three sections for convenient transportation and to facilitate repairs to the body. Damage to one section of a three-piece body is easier to deal with than damage to a one-piece body. A three-piece body can easily have a damaged section replaced without replacing the entire body.

In determining who invented the oboe, we can only guess based on word-of-mouth evidence from individuals in Europe's music world of the seventeenth-century era. Some historians credit Jean Hotteterre and Michel Danican Philidor as the inventors, separately or together.

The instrument known as the hautbois was a modification of the Shawm. The windcap was replaced by a double reed, and gradually, a key system evolved to accommodate the needs of the music. Four stages of development followed this. These were labeled Baroque, Classical, Viennese, and Conservatory models.

The original Baroque oboe was a simple instrument with three keys ranging from C4 to D6. To move to a higher register, the player had to increase the intensity of the air stream.

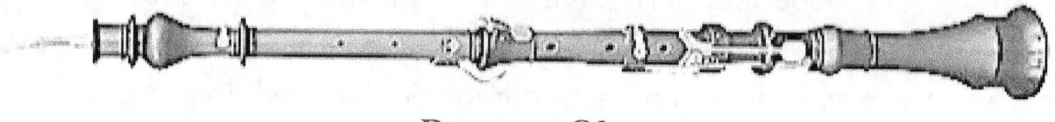

Baroque Oboe

During the classical period in music, a more advanced oboe was developed to satisfy the growing needs of the music performance community. The instrument had additional keys, a decreased bore diameter to ease playing in the upper register, and a vent key (not quite an octave key as we know it), which easily shifted up an octave. It was later in evolution that a true octave key was devised. The classical oboe range increased to F6.

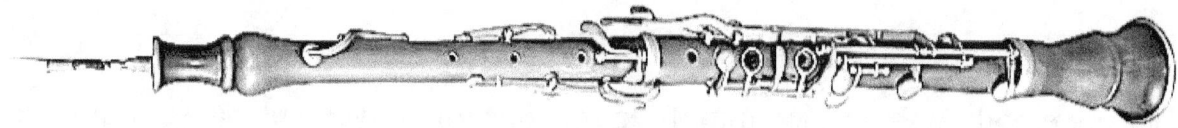

Classical Oboe

The Viennese oboe began appearing in the last quarter of the nineteenth century. This is a hybrid of oboes from the Austrian/German system with a larger bore and a more complex key system. The upper register was also stronger in timbre and projection due to increased upper partials. The larger bore, combined with wider and shorter reeds, produces a strong, double-reed sound with ease of playing. Note the differently shaped bell. The Viennese oboe might be considered the bridge from the antique to today's instrument. This instrument is still in use today.

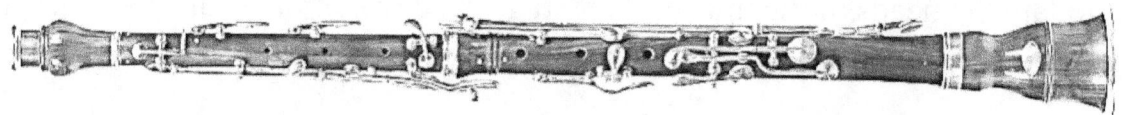

Viennese Oboe

The conservatory oboe was also developed at about the same time as the Viennese oboe and had a key system modeled after the Boehm oboe system. This system was not very popular but did act as the next step in developing the instrument to reach the point of the modern full conservatory system now in use. The full conservatory system has forty-five keys, some with rings and others with plateau keys. These oboes have a range from Bb3 to A6.

Conservatory Oboe

The modern oboe is the one in use today. It is the product of all that preceded it, with an excellent but complex key system and bore dimensions that produce the oboe sound we all recognize. This general design is now made in many different models to satisfy the entire range of notes used in music today.

Modern Oboe

The Bassoon

The Bassoon—The Shawm, dulcian, and rankett are considered the forerunners of the bassoon. These instruments were popular for about two hundred years from the mid-sixteenth century. Like the bassoon, they used a double reed connected to a bocal. As the double reed shawm (described above) evolved into larger sizes, producing lower pitches, we could consider it the beginning of what would eventually become the bassoon.

The dulcian was a step closer to our current bassoon. Its bore was cone-shaped and long enough to be folded upon itself. However, unlike the bassoon, the dulcian was carved from one piece of maple.

The tone holes had to be drilled at an angle so that on the inside of the bore, they were placed according to the sound requirements, while on the outside of the instrument, they would fit a normal finger span of the player.

During the Dulcian period of popularity, eight different-sized versions were developed to complete the soprano to bass range. The instrument had eight tone holes and two keys. The dulcian continued to be popular as the bassoon began to make its appearance.

Dulcian

The rankett was also an instrument from the sixteenth century that may have added to the development of the bassoon in that the rankett was a double reed instrument with a range as low as G2.

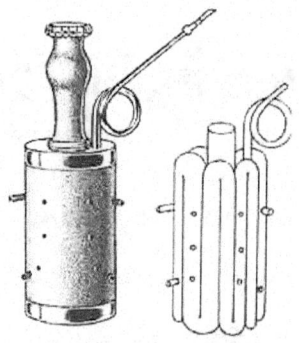

Rankett
(Compliments of Wikipedia)

The unique difference was that rather than having a straight bore found in other woodwind instruments, the rankett was about five inches long but achieved the low range through a cylindrical bore within the body with nine tone holes spaced to accommodate the spread of a player's hand.

Other modifications in the tone holes and bore made by John Christian Denner are described above as having advanced the technology of the chalumeau to the point where he made the first extended-range baroque bassoon. He developed the rankett to the point where it was, in effect, a small bassoon.

Jacques Martin Hotteterre (1673–1763), as mentioned above, Jacques devised the oboe with a three-piece design with a separate head joint, body, and foot joint structure. In addition to being a prominent flutist, composer, and Renaissance man in the music world of his time, he is credited with being one of several individuals responsible for developing the bassoon.

As a member of a large family of instrument makers, we might guess that Hotteterre was able to use his musical ability, experience, and creativity in conjunction with the skills of his instrument-maker family members to develop and build an early bassoon. Hotteterre increased the bell's size, extending the bassoon's range, and he designed the instrument in four sections so the bore could be more accurately machined.

Carl Almenraeder (1786–1846) is credited with designing a bassoon with 17 keys that could play a four-octave range chromatically. Almenraeder joined J.A. Heckel (1812–1877) in producing what would become the German Heckel system bassoon. Heckel went on to expand the bassoon range and create a contrabassoon. Both of these were prototypes for the bassoons used today.

The advancement of technology in musical instrument manufacturing and an increased understanding of the principles of acoustics enabled instrument makers to provide for the increased demands of the performing community. And so evolved the Heckle or German system and the Buffet or French system bassoons. These are two distinctly different instruments that, to date, serve two differing viewpoints on what a bassoon should be.

The Heckel (German) system features a more complicated key system with up to 27 keys joined with a wider bore, producing a fuller sound. Heckel system bassoons currently enjoy popularity throughout most of the world, while the Buffet model has greater popularity in France, Spain, and Canada.

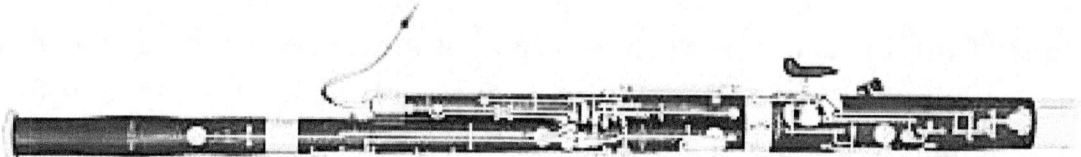

Heckel System Bassoon

The Buffet (French) design has a simple 22-key system joined with a narrow bore. The results are less complicated fingering requirements and a more lyrical mellow tone quality.

Buffet System Bassoon

Summary—The early history of woodwind instruments is, at best, vague and lacking in definitive structure. As far as we know, they began with the simple act of blowing air into some reed-like plant. Yet, they became more complex mechanically and acoustically than all the other instruments.

Because there is a shortage of documentation on the early phase of woodwind instrument history, it is necessary to guess their development. From Medieval times to the present, organologists (musical instrument scientists) have access to an almost overwhelming amount of documented history on how woodwind instruments began to be crafted and developed to the point at which we now enjoy their use.

The instruments of the woodwind family provide the music community with a listening pleasure that spans most of the notes with any emotion, from expressive lyricism to dynamic brilliance. These instruments can stand on their own as solo instruments, be part of a woodwind ensemble, or contribute to the sounds of any other combination of musical instruments. In a symphony orchestra, they are the core of the auditory transition between the string and brass sections.

From the primitive individuals who made the first sounds with a bamboo reed to the inventors, musicians, technicians, and visionaries who brought us up to the point where society is now fortunate enough to enjoy a listening experience that has become a precious possession of our music world, a profound thank you!

NOTES

Chapter 8

What Items (Accessories) Will I Need to Help Me Play My Flute?

An accessory is something that will help you use your flute but is not part of a basic flute outfit. The descriptions and pictures of accessories below are just some of these items. You can find hundreds more on the Internet.

To function properly, musical instruments require accessories. Three categories of accessories available are used to support the playing experience: those that are necessary, those that make playing easier and maintain an instrument, and those that are luxuries.

The following accessories are needed to successfully play and maintain any of the instruments in the flute family. Because of the many brands of each product on the market, I will discuss this topic in general terms.

Lubricants—Flutes have many moving parts which require regular lubrication. Searching for "flute lubricants" in Google Images will illustrate the variety of available products. The following is a description of different types of lubricants and their use.

Selecting Key Oil—To decide how long an oil will work successfully on your flute keys before evaporating, rub a drop of oil between your thumb and index finger and judge how long the oily sensation lasts. Compare several oils against one another. Petroleum-based oils will probably last a shorter time than synthetic oils. The choice of oil is a very individual one.

Light oil evaporates more quickly than thicker oils. Light oil tends to travel down the post to the instrument's body. This is messy and will collect dust.

To test the viscosity (thickness) of oil, start by shaking the bottle to see how the contents move. The slower the oil moves, the thicker it is.

In chapter 5, you learned how to compare the thickness of several oils by placing a drop of each, side by side, on one end of a smooth, flat surface. Then, raise that end of the surface and note the rate of speed at which the oils travel downward. Thicker oils will move more slowly. With several choices, try each on one key of your flute using a different key for each trial. Do not combine different oils during the trial.

Using Oil—The figure below shows key oil in a needle-type dispenser for easy distribution. The oil you use for each process will have to be your decision. Use the following information to start your search on the subject. Note the oils that are packaged with a needle applicator. Those are very convenient.

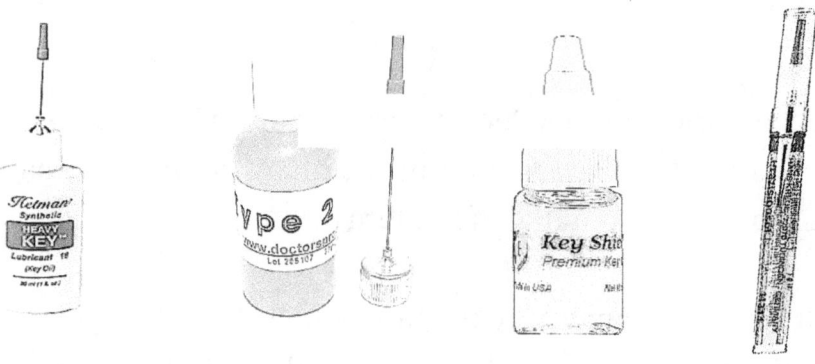

Key Oil

Cork Grease—Chapter 5 taught you how to use cork grease to lubricate the cork in your flute's crown assembly. There are many brands of cork grease available. Again, ask your teacher for advice on which kind to use. Below are four different packagings of cork grease.

Cork Grease Packagings

Cleaning Brushes—Flute key cleaning brushes are available in many shapes and sizes. Below are three examples. Your local music store or an online search will show you many more. Choose the ones you feel will best serve your needs.

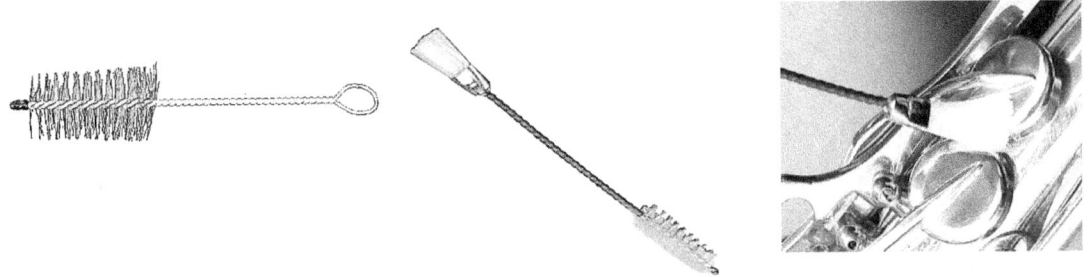

Flute Key Cleaning Brushes

Electronic Tuners—An electronic tuner can be used to check if you are playing in tune. With certain models, you can play a note, and a needle on a screen will show you if the sound is sharp, flat, or on pitch. You can adjust the instrument or your embouchure until the correct pitch is reached. Below are two chromatic electronic tuners with a screen and a clip-on model showing if the note sounding is in tune, sharp, or flat. Search Google images "tuners for a flute," and you will see more.

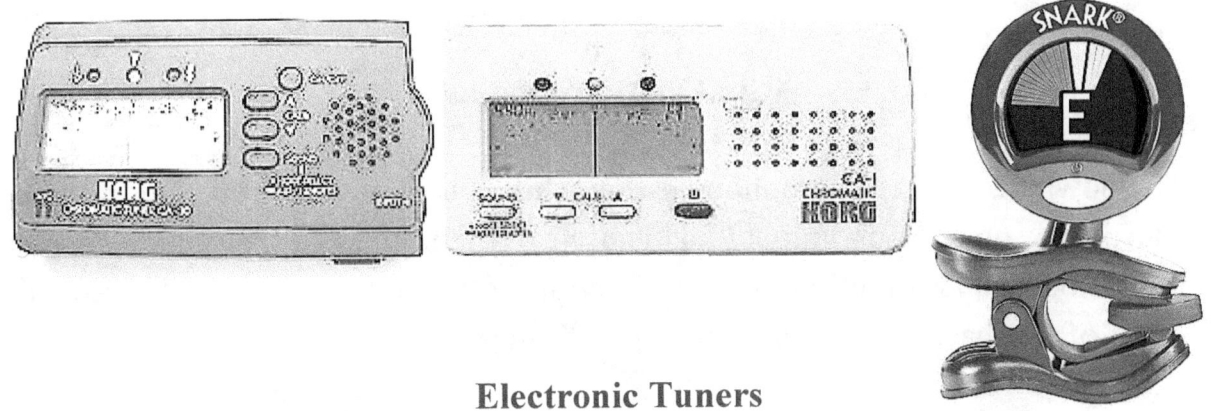

Electronic Tuners

Apps or Applications—You can find help tuning on websites, cell phones, iPads, the Internet, and other Wi-Fi devices.

Acoustic Electric Instruments—An amplified flute is a traditional flute to which a pickup (microphone) is added. Two kinds of pickups in general use are a microphone in various locations depending on the instrument and a magnetic pickup, which is usually connected directly to your flute's head joint. The pickups are connected with a cable to an amplifier using the same equipment used for the electric guitar.

The condenser microphone is most popular because of its low cost and true sound. This microphone converts sound waves into electrical energy and sends them to an amplifier, which sends them to a speaker. A condenser microphone can easily be clipped onto almost any instrument, and you have an amplified (electric) instrument.

The pickup you choose can be connected to a pre-amplifier, amplifier, equalizer, and speaker. With the proper equipment, the pickup can also be wireless. The pictures below show three different kinds of microphones that can be used on flutes. There are many more.

Clip On Microphones

The downside to this microphone is that while it will pick up your flute sound, it will also pick up surrounding sounds caused by handling the instrument, such as bumps, knocks, and sometimes even the action of the keys in motion. There is also a danger of feedback when using this type of microphone.

The term used to define this type of microphone is cardioid, which can pick up sound from an area of 180 degrees from the front with fading reception beyond that radius.

Another condenser microphone is the piezoelectric microphone, which receives vibrations through direct contact with the instrument. This type of pickup is placed on your flute, where it will pick up the total quality of the sound.

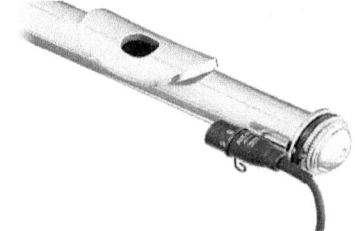

Direct Contact Microphone

Music Stands—Using a music stand when you practice will help you keep the correct posture and playing position. There are stands that fold, others that do not fold, and tabletop versions. A folding stand is lightweight, portable, and very inexpensive. Most beginning students use it.

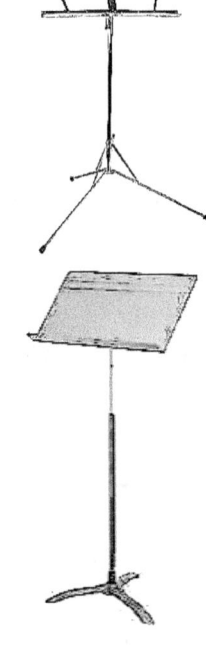

A non-folding rigid stand called the concert, stage, or orchestra music stand is not easy to carry and is often used in one place. It is more expensive than the folding stand but is very stable, able to hold a large amount of music, and is very sturdy. The cost of this stand usually ranges from two to four times that of a folding stand.

A tabletop stand is small, portable, without legs, lightweight and inexpensive. It can be placed on any stable surface and allows complete flexibility. Below are pictures of decorative, folding, and non-folding tabletop stands.

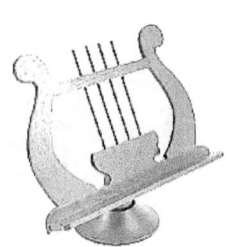 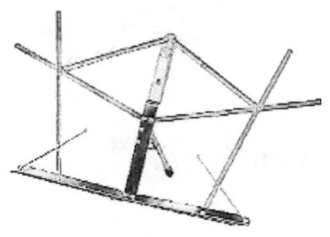 

Tabletop Music Stands

Swabs—Swabs are needed to dry your flute's bore (inside) after playing. Below are pictured a stick swab, a flute cleaning rod onto which you place a cloth, a pull-through swab, a swab with a microfiber cloth with an extended weighted pull-through cord, and a double chord back-and-forth pull-through swab.

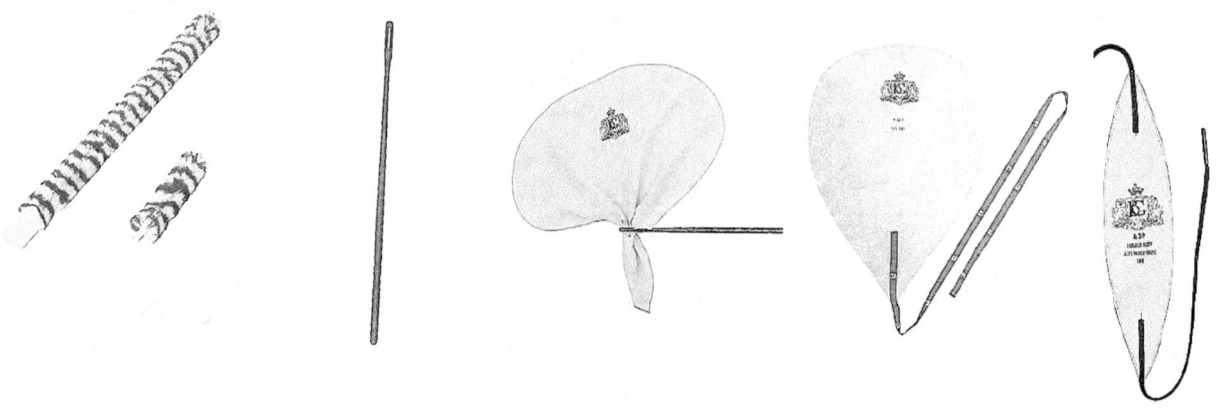

Flute Swabs

Look online for a style you think will work for you, find it in a music store, try it, and if you like it, make the swab yours.

Lyres—A lyre is a portable music stand used to hold music for marching band instruments. Below are three kinds of lyres used for a flute or piccolo. The first is a clip-on (Grover), the next is a wrist strap (Gottfried), and the last is an under-arm model (Riedl).

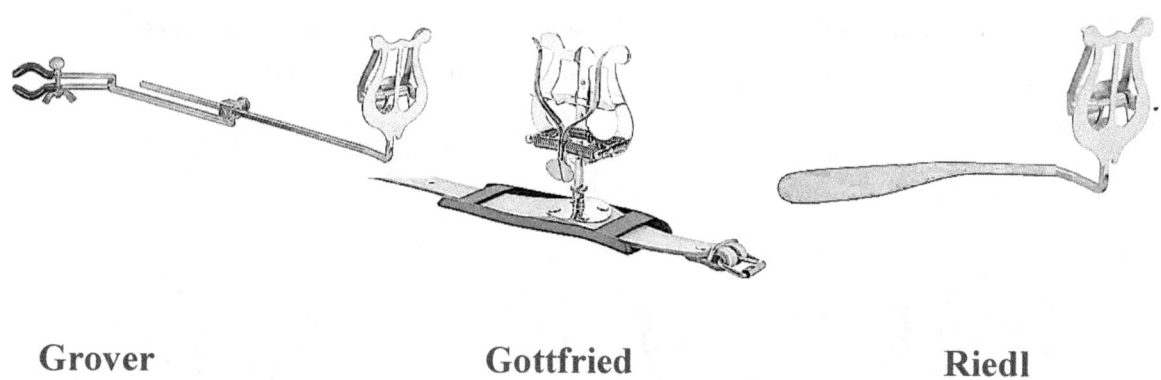

Grover   **Gottfried**   **Riedl**

Flute Stands—There are stands designed to hold flutes safely when not in use. Before buying a stand, search "flute stands" on Google Images, click on the picture of the one you like best, then click "visit page" for more information. You can order it online or print the page and try your local music store. The pictures below show a variety of stands that hold several different instruments.

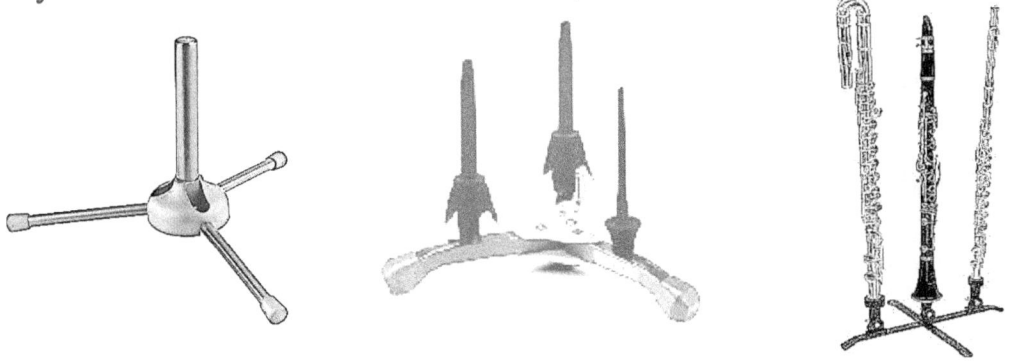

Single Flute **Clarinet/Flute/Piccolo** **Alto Flute/Clarinet/Flute**

Flute Stands

Flute Cases—Flute cases can be made with a hard or soft body. Hard cases are usually heavier than soft cases but offer more protection for your instrument. Soft cases are often called "gig bags." If they are padded, they will provide protection for normal use. You should use a hard case if you plan to travel or tend to be rough with your instrument. Below are pictures of some hard and soft cases. A simple "Google Images" search for flute cases will show many more.

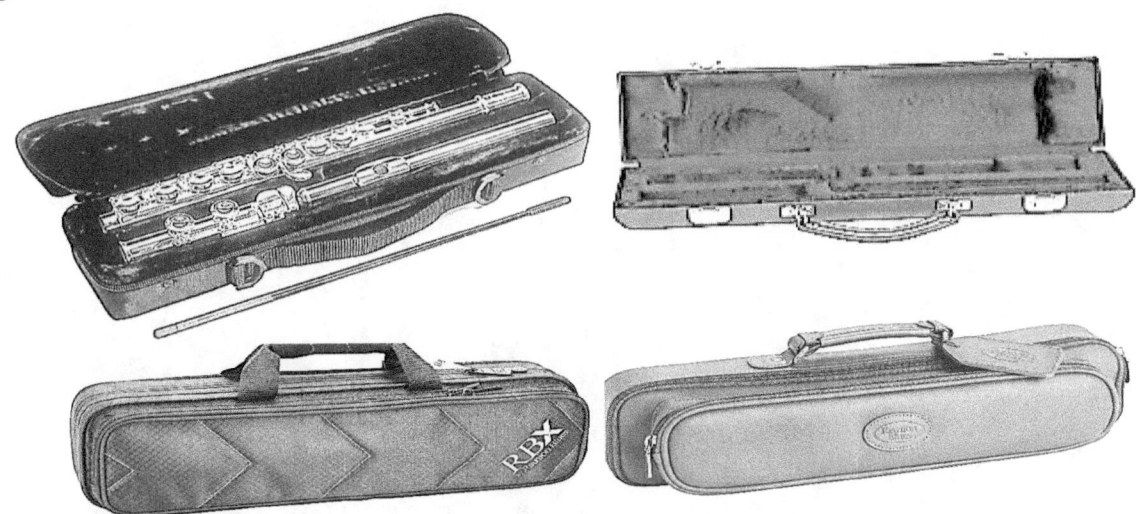

Flute Cases

Summary—The examples of flute accessories shown in this chapter are just a few of what is available for each item. There are hundreds more that you can find with a simple online search. As you progress in your studies, at some point, you will find that there were accessories you did not have when you began your studies, but that will help you advance your playing skills and keep your flute in good playing condition. Choose wisely, ask for advice from your teacher and other professionals, and search online for those items you feel will help you play better.

Appendix

Note: In this appendix, you will learn words used in the study of the science of sound. When these words appear, they will be followed by the more common term in parentheses.

Scientific Pitch Notation—The following explains a system used throughout music study called *Scientific Pitch Notation*. This is a valuable tool that can serve you throughout your music career.

Scientific Pitch Notation helps you know exactly where a note is located on the staff without seeing the note in print. This system uses alphanumerics (a combination of letters and numerals) to tell you exactly where a note is in the entire range of notes. An example would be middle C, whose alphanumeric name is C4. The C one octave below middle C is C3. The C an octave above middle C is C5. The notes going up between these Cs keep the C's numeral until the next C is reached. Examples would be C4, D4, E4, F4, G4, A4, B4, C5, D5, etc. The figure below shows the alphanumeric symbol for all notes.

Scientific Pitch Notation

Sound—Sound occurs when something causes vibrations in the air. The vibrations travel by waves of air pushed against one another, acting as a train would when the last car is pushed, and each car moves in front of the last one. This is called a chain reaction.

Molecules (tiny bits) of air push against one another to make sound travel. The grouping of tight molecules pictured below is named compression. The more open pattern is called rarefaction.

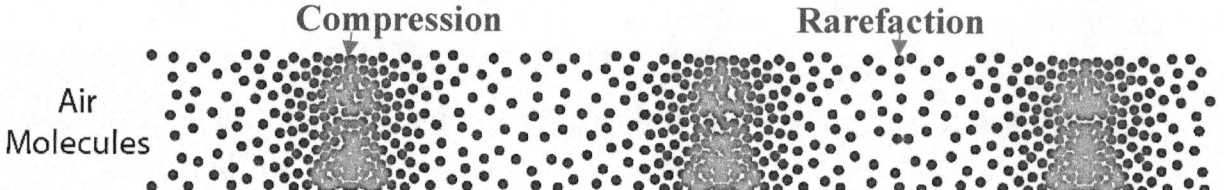

The combined action of compression and rarefaction results in a complete cycle of sound.

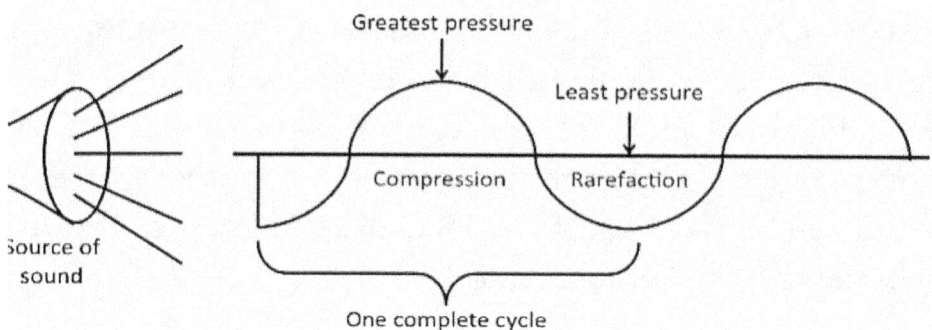

Vibration—If you look very closely at a guitar string that has been plucked, you will see that it moves very rapidly from side to side.

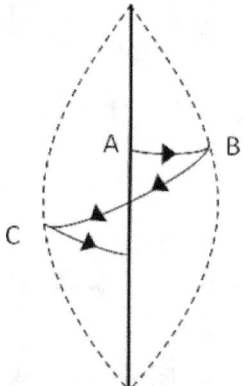

It moves from the center (A) to one side (B) and back across the center (A) to the other side (C). This entire voyage completes *one cycle*.

Cycles per Second (cps) or Hertz (Hz), named after the physicist Heinrich Hertz, refers to the number of complete cycles per second, so 30 Hz means 30 cycles per second. Any tone results from the number of vibrations or cycles per second. "A" 440 is the tone produced by an instrument producing 440 vibrations or cycles per second. Below are some examples of notes with their cps.

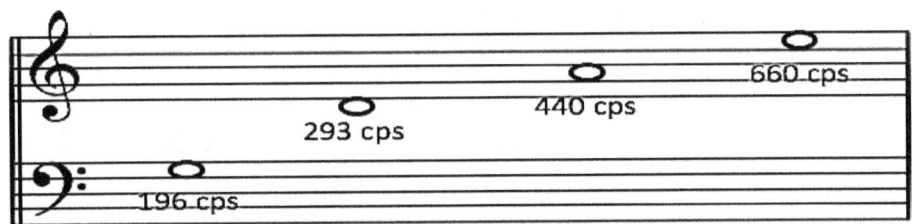

Cycles per Second

Sine Wave—When sound is created on a musical instrument, it produces a pattern of vibrations. These vibrations include a fundamental (basic) pitch and several other related pitches with less amplitude (volume). The fundamental pitch alone is a *pure tone* and can be pictured as a simple wave.

Pure Tone

Amplitude—Amplitude refers to the volume or loudness of a sound. Greater amplitude produces louder sounds. Less amplitude produces softer sounds.

Harmonics—When a tone is produced on a flute, it is joined by a series of related sounds or tones called harmonics. Other terms used for harmonics are overtones or upper partials. Any of these three terms can be used. Harmonics (overtones or upper partials) are less important vibrations sounding with the fundamental (basic pitch) but with less amplitude (volume).

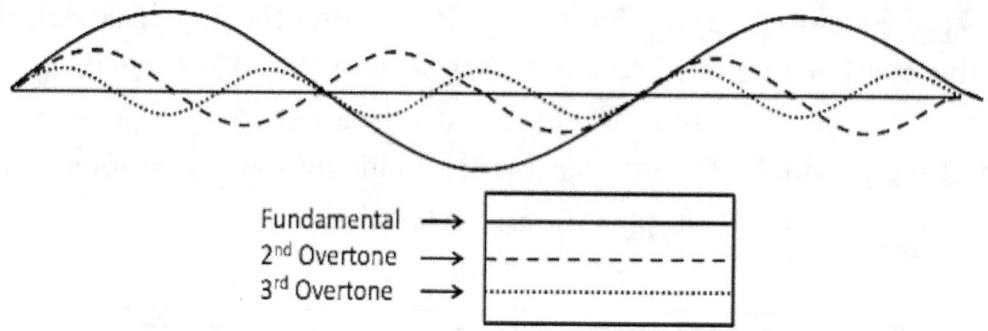

Harmonics cannot be heard as notes but are additions to the fundamental (basic pitch). Combining a basic pitch with harmonics results in the pitches' timbre (total sound).

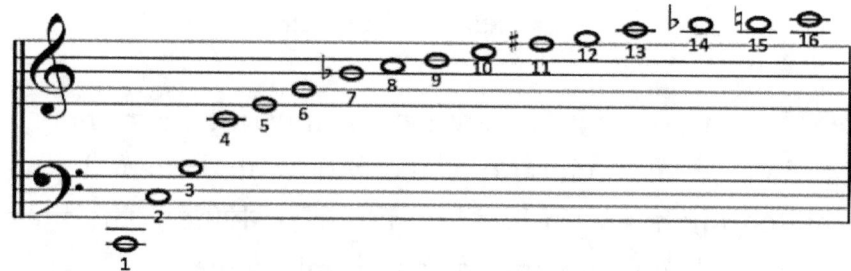

Harmonic Sequence

Timbre—Timbre is the product of adding tones to a fundamental pitch. These additional sounds, referred to as harmonics (overtones or upper partials), result from the built-in sound features of the instrument producing the sound. For the note C, these sounds follow the harmonic sequence pictured above and are present in most tones. The same interval pattern would occur for any note.

The difference in timbre results from the amplitude of the harmonics and how they relate in volume to the fundamental pitch. Stronger harmonics produce a timbre of greater intensity. Less amplitude of the harmonics will produce a less intense timbre. Tones played on the oboe have strong harmonics, producing a tone that can be identified as having an intense timbre. On the other hand, the flute has a comparatively weak set of harmonics and produces a more mellow tone.

Tone is a combination of pitch, volume, and timbre (the special quality of a pitch).

Pitch is the highness or lowness of a tone. The notes of an ascending scale (do, re, mi, fa, sol, la, ti, do) go up in pitch or are successively higher. The notes going down in pitch are successively lower in a descending scale (do, ti, la, sol, fa, mi, re, do).

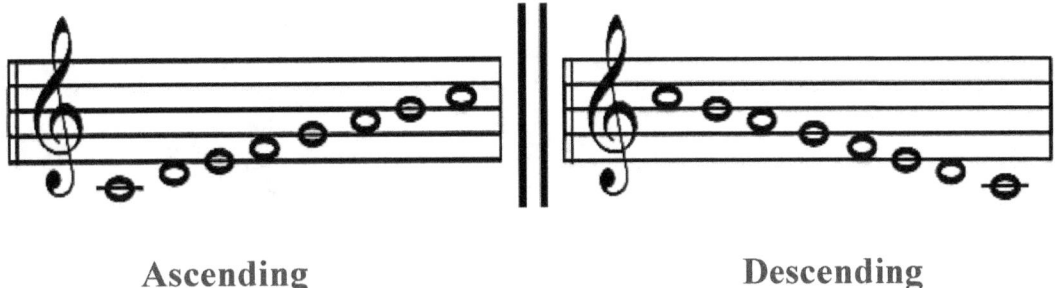

Ascending　　　　　　　　　　Descending

Any series of notes can take one of only three possible directions in pitch. They can ascend (A), descend (B), or remain the same (C).

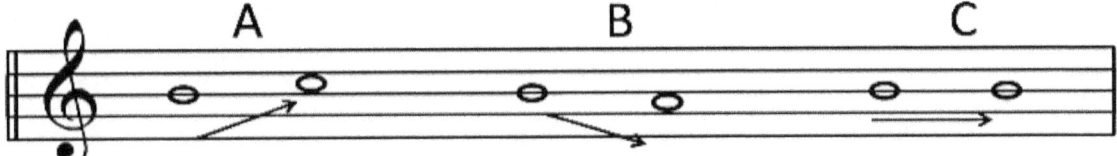

Summary—As you study your instrument, you are learning how to read music, use that information to work the mechanics of your flute to produce sounds, and then, using your artistic sense, turn those sounds into music. A terrific achievement. However, there is an underlying study that is not usually given much attention. That is the study of sound.

The chapter you just read gives you a very slight overview of some of the many topics in that subject. You learned words like scientific pitch notation, vibrations, compression, rarefaction, cycles per second, tone, amplitude, and harmonics. Those are just a few topics in the study of sound.

As you progress in your flute studies, include some of these sound topics, and you will be able to apply that knowledge to your music performance and be a better, more knowledgeable musician.

NOTES

Glossary of Woodwind Instrument Terms

Adjustment Screws—a screw used to adjust key systems.

Alphasax—a redesigned saxophone for smaller players.

Annealing—applying heat to brass to change its shape.

Aulos—an ancient Greek flute-like instrument found in Greek art.

Baffle—the lower part of the reed side of a single reed mouthpiece.

Baroque—a decorative performance style or any art form practiced during the seventeenth and eighteenth centuries.

Barrel—the first section of a clarinet after the mouthpiece.

Bass Joint—the section of a bassoon located between the boot and bell joints.

Bell—the lowest section of a clarinet, saxophone, oboe, or bassoon.

Bell Joint—the last section of a bassoon.

Billet—a section of wood in the first stages of a woodwind instrument construction.

Boot Joint—the second and lowest section of a bassoon body.

Bore—the inner tube of a musical instrument in which the vibrating column of air becomes a tone.

Chalumeau—the precursor to the clarinet and the name of its lowest range.

Clarinet—a category of single reed cylindrical bore woodwind instruments.

Clarineo Lyons C Clarinet—A lightweight model of the Bb clarinet designed for young students.

Classical Music—Music composed during the eighteenth and nineteenth century.

Closed Hole—a woodwind instrument key with a pad covering a tone hole.

Conservatory System—one of three key systems on an oboe.

Contrabassoon—a lower-pitched version of a bassoon.

Cork Pads—pads made of cork used on woodwind instrument keys.

Crown—the first section of a flute head joint.

Crumhorn—a double reed woodwind windcap instrument from the Renaissance period.

Double Reed—a two-bladed reed used without a mouthpiece on instruments in the oboe and bassoon families.

Ebonite—a manmade hard rubber product used to make woodwind instrument bodies.

Facing—the upper segment of the reed side of a single reed mouthpiece.

Finger—(see paddle) the section of a woodwind key where the player's finger is applied.

Fingering—the pattern used on the keys of a woodwind instrument to play a note.

Fish Skin Pads—fish skin used to cover the contact surface of some woodwind instrument pads.

Flat Shelf—the edge shelf section of a flute head joint embouchure hole.

Flat Spring—one of three types of springs used to return a key to its rest position.

Fulcrum—the pivot point on a woodwind instrument key.

Fundamental—the basic pitch upon which overtones are built.

Grenadilla—a close-grained, dark-colored, dense wood used to make woodwind instrument bodies.

Harmonics—pitches related to a fundamental pitch but sounding in lesser degrees of volume.

Head Joint— the first section of a flute. A head joint has an embouchure hole into which the player blows air to produce a sound.

Intonation—the degree of accuracy with which a pitch is produced. A note can be in tune, sharp, or flat.

Key Pad Cup—the part of a woodwind key into which a pad is placed to cover a tone hole.

Key Springs—springs made of wire, blue steel, or other alloys installed to return a woodwind key to its original point of rest.

Key System—an arrangement of keys on a woodwind instrument.

Kinder Klari—a small E-flat clarinet modified to ease use by small hands.

Lay—(facing) the upper section of the reed side of a single reed mouthpiece.

Leather Pads—leather in place of fish skin used to surface the contact side of a woodwind instrument key pad.

Ligature—a band of metal or other material used to hold a reed on a single reed mouthpiece.

Lower Joint—the lower section of the body of a clarinet or oboe.

Mouthpiece—the first part of the single reed woodwind instrument into which the player will blow to produce sound.

Neck—the uppermost section of a saxophone onto which the mouthpiece is connected.

Oboe—a double reed woodwind instrument with a range of about two octaves producing tones strong in upper partials.

Open Hole—a woodwind instrument key with a cup with a hole in its center.

Pad—a soft, fish skin or leather padded disc in woodwind instrument key pad cups that make contact with and seal tone holes.

Paddle—the part of a woodwind key that the player's finger contacts.

Pitch—the highness or lowness of a tone.

Plateau Keys—keys that fully cover a tone hole.

Posts—knob-like elements holding the keys onto the body of a woodwind instrument.

Professional Level—the highest quality musical instrument.

Reed—a formed strip of cane used as a sound generator on woodwind instruments.

Resonator—a hard surfaced disc added to the center of a key pad to increase the resonance of a woodwind instrument.

Resonite—acrylonitrile butadiene styrene (ABS) used to make bodies for inexpensive woodwind instruments.

Rib Construction—a strip of metal used to reinforce posts on flutes and saxophones.

Rosewood—a beautifully grained, lighter-colored wood used to make clarinet and oboe bodies.

Saxonette—a clarinet-like instrument with a neck and upturned bell used as a transitional instrument between the clarinet and saxophone.

Saxophone—a single reed, brass-bodied woodwind instrument with padded keys.

Scientific Pitch Notation—an alphanumeric system combining letters and numbers to identify the location of a note on the staff.

Shawm—the wind-capped predecessor to the oboe, popular in the Medieval and Renaissance periods.

Side Rails—the two narrow sides of a single reed mouthpiece bore.

Silicon Pads—a durable pad with a silicon surface used on woodwind instruments.

Single-Reed Mouthpiece—a mouthpiece designed to use a single reed, typically for a clarinet or saxophone.

Sonic Welding—high-frequency sound waves used to install posts on plastic instrument bodies.

Sound Production—the process unique to each instrument used to generate sound.

Spatula—the fingered part of a woodwind instrument key.

Spring—strips of various metal alloys used to return a woodwind instrument key to its rest position.

Staple—the cork-covered tubular bottom of a double reed inserted into an instrument.

Step-Up (Intermediate)—the next step up in quality and workmanship from a student-level musical instrument.

Student-Level—the least expensive entry-level musical instrument.

Tenon—the projection that joins each section of a woodwind instrument.

Throat—the inner section of a single reed mouthpiece between the chamber and the bore.

Tip Rail—the rounded top edge of the window of a single reed mouthpiece.

Tone Holes—holes in the body of a woodwind instrument used to change pitches.

Transposition—changing any combination of notes to a different key.

Triple Reed—a reed with three blades.

Tuning—the act of adjusting the pitch of an instrument.

Upper Joint—the upper section of the body of a woodwind instrument.

Windcap—a cylinder that encloses a double reed.

Window—the opening between the rails of a single reed mouthpiece.

Wing Joint—the first section of a bassoon's body after the bocal.

Zummara—a two-bodied mid-eastern woodwind instrument.

NOTES

Dictionary of Flute Terms

For your convenience, this dictionary is a review of flute-only terms taken from the woodwind glossary above.

Bore—the flute's inner tube in which the air's vibrating column becomes a tone.

Finger—(see paddle) the section of a key where the player's finger is applied.

Fingering—the pattern used by your fingers on the keys of a flute to play a note.

Fish Skin Pads—pads with fish skin covering their contact surface.

Flat Spring—one of three types of springs used to return a key to its rest position.

Intonation—the degree of correctness of a pitch. A note can be in tune, sharp, or flat.

Key Pad Cup—the part of a flute key with a pad covering a tone hole.

Key Springs—springs made of wire, blue steel, or other alloys on a flute key to return it to its original point of rest.

Key System—an arrangement of keys on a flute.

Pad—a soft fish skin or leather padded disc in flute key pad cups that contact and seal tone holes.

Paddle—the finger part of a flute key.

Pitch—the highness or lowness of a tone.

Plateau Keys—keys that fully cover a tone hole.

Posts—supports on a flute's body holding the keys.

Professional Level—the most expensive, highest quality flute

Silicon Pads—a durable pad with a silicon surface used on flute keys.

Sound Production—the process used to produce sound.

Spatula—the fingered part of a flute key.

Spring—strips of metal alloys used to return a flute key to its rest position.

Step-Up (Intermediate)—the next step up in quality and workmanship from a student-level flute.

Student Level—the least expensive entry-level flute.

Tenon—the projection that joins each section of a flute.

Tone Holes—holes in the body of a flute that you can open or close to change pitches.

Transposition—changing any combination of notes to a different key.

Tuning—the act of adjusting the pitch of a flute.

Index of Flute Parts

Use this index to see pages on actual flute parts.

Body, 1

Crown, 2

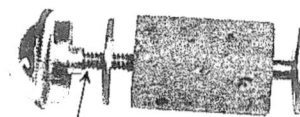

Fish Skin Pad, 76

Foot Joint, 1

Head Joint, 1

Key Pad Cup, 14, 23

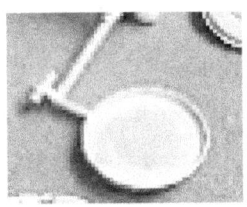

Key Springs, 3

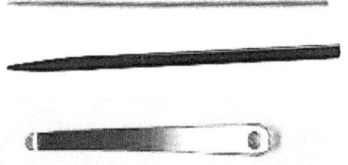

wire, needle, flat

Key System, 8

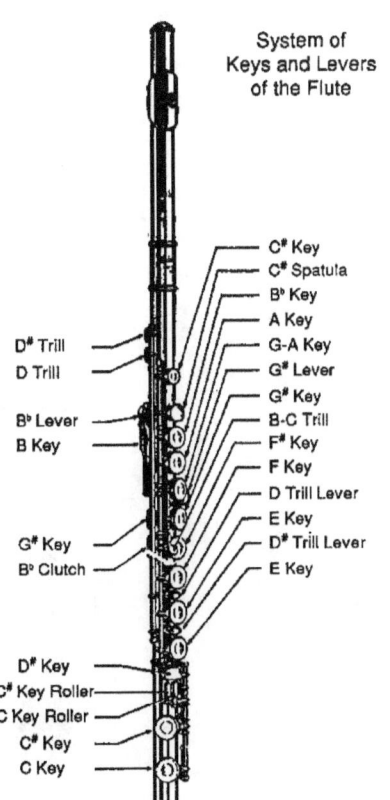

Open Hole Flute Keys, 3

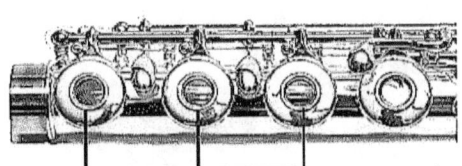

Paddle, 77

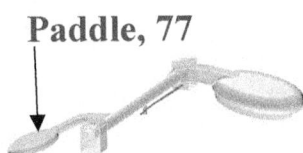

83

Plateau Keys, 3

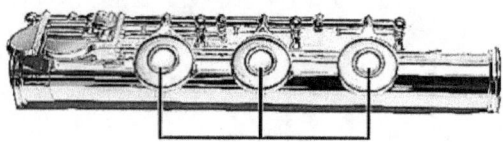

Posts, 2

Tenon, 79, 82

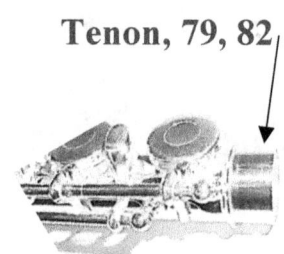

Tone Hole, 2

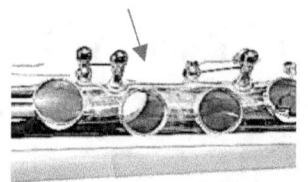

Instrument Ownership Record

This diary is designed to document the history and maintenance of your flute. By entering all the relevant information regularly, you will have a reference for periodic maintenance, information for a possible sale in the future, and a history of the instrument. Not every category listed will be relevant to every instrument. Fill in relevant information and add any other information that suits your situation.

(Instrument) _____

Instrument's History

Owner's name _____

Date of purchase _____

Where purchased _____

Brand _____

Model _____

Date made _____

New [ ] previously owned [ ] Check one.

Previous owner(s) name(s) _____

Identifying marks, labels, serial number _____

Seller's Information

Name_____

Address_____

Phone_____

Email_____

Website_____

List or asking price_____

Price paid_____

NOTES

Maintenance Record

When making an entry, include the date, action, repair, replacement or service, part serviced, brand or description of replacement part, source, technician's name, and contact information. Keep all invoices in a file for future reference.

General Service

DATE	SERVICE	TECHNICIAN	COST

Major Repairs

Detail the date, damage, cause, how it was repaired, by whom, and cost.

DATE	DESCRIBE REPAIR	COST	TECHNICIAN

Index

adjustment screws, 75
aulos, 43, 75
Baroque, 41, 53–54, 57, 75
Bassoon, 43, 55–58, 75–76, 79
bore, 26–28, 32, 42, 44, 48, 51–52, 54–58, 66, 75, 78–79, 81
care, 25–34
cases, 67
chalumeau, 44–46, 57, 75
clarinet, 11, 43–49, 75, 77–78
classical, 42, 45, 51–54, 75
closed hole, 3, 7, 75
crown, 2, 6, 26–27, 62, 76, 83
conservatory system, 53, 55, 75
crumhorn, 44-45, 76
dulcian, 55–56
fingering, 7, 9–11, 14, 44, 47–49, 58, 76
fipple, 41
fish skin, 76–77, 81, 83
flat spring, 3, 76, 81
flute (history), 39–43
harmonics, 71–73, 76
history, 39–59
Hotteterre, 40, 53, 57
Intonation, 35, 37, 40, 42, 44–48, 52–53, 76, 81
key pad cup, 14, 77, 81, 83
key springs, 3, 32, 77, 81, 83
key system, 7–8, 17, 23, 31, 40, 46–49, 53–55, 58, 75, 77, 81, 83

made, (flute) 17–23
mouthpiece, 47-52, 75–79
oboe, 52–55
open hole, 3, 7, 14, 77, 83
ophicleide, 49
pad, 2–3, 7, 19, 22–23, 28, 32–33, 46–47, 49, 75–78, 81, 83
paddle, 77, 81, 83
pitch, 4–6, 40. 43–45, 47, 55, 63, 69, 71–73, 75–79, 81–82
plateau keys, 3, 14, 55, 77, 81, 84
posts, 2, 19, 30–31, 77–78, 81–84
rib construction, 78
saxophone, 49–52
shawm, 52–55, 78
silicon, 78, 81
sound production, 5, 78, 81
spatula, 2, 78, 81
spring, 2–3, 28, 32–33, 76–77, 79–83
step-up, 79, 82
student-level, 4, 79, 82
tenon, 79, 82, 84
tone holes, 2–3, 5, 7, 17–19, 22–23, 32–33, 39–41, 43, 45–49, 52, 56–57, 75, 77, 79, 81–82, 84
transposition, 11, 79, 82
tuning, 2, 6, 27–28, 63, 79, 82
windcap, 44–45, 52-53, 76, 79
zummara, 44, 79

www.ingramcontent.com/pod-product-compliance
Lightning Source LLC
Chambersburg PA
CBHW081847230426
43669CB00018B/2852